BULLIED

The Horror and the Strength Within

LOU ENZO MAYSON

iUniverse®

BULLIED
THE HORROR AND THE STRENGTH WITHIN

iUniverse books may be ordered through booksellers or by contacting:

iUniverse
1663 Liberty Drive
Bloomington, IN 47403
www.iuniverse.com
1-800-Authors (1-800-288-4677)

ISBN: 978-1-5320-6332-9 (sc)
ISBN: 978-1-5320-6334-3 (hc)
ISBN: 978-1-5320-6333-6 (e)

Print information available on the last page.

iUniverse rev. date: 01/14/2019

INTRODUCTION

When you drive or walk city streets these days and you see a

a homeless person with a sign that says various things, things that

cause most of us to react differently. Some of us call 'em lazy and

hopeless. Others reach into our pockets for coins, maybe even a
buck

or two. Very few people take into account and wonder what
brought

that soul to dip that low and end up that impoverished in the U.S.

This book is about two children that were raised in a very

unstable environment. I do want you to rest assured, that, this is

fact based, there is nothing exaggerated nor truth stretched in any

way. I also want my readers to understand that I am not attempting

to seek sympathy for anyone, including myself. This is a
collection of

story's in an, easy to read book, written in a way to inform
children,

adults and parents of ways to deal with the inevitable in the face of

people with insecurities. Everything in this book actually happened. I

survived it. I lived it. Now, I am sharing it.

I've been involved in several scenarios with the paranormal

beginning at a surprisingly young age. I, of course, would never claim

to know about the here after. I just happened to be in a place where

the opportunity presented it self to give me a choice to question fact

or fiction.

With all this said, I should inform you that I am one to cut

to the chase. I surely don't care to bore an audience with a bunch of

unnecessary detail. You will agree, that, in the end, I surely did not

need to fudge or stretch subjects to keep anyone riveted. Most of us

have struggled down the rocky road, called life. I am probably

putting down on paper and defining what *you* have seen, and or, ex-

perienced yourself. You just haven't gotten around to writing a book about it. A lot of adults have got several horror stories to tell about

being bullied in their adolescence. I'm sharing mostly my winnings,

so, I can break through to readers without sounding like I lost the

battle. Let me tell ya baby, battle is over, but the war goes on!

Believe me, it took a lifetime of many harsh realities to

finally get to the place where a person like me is receptive to real

love, and understanding the unconditional love. Thus, I have learned

to think in practical terms in every approach when dealing with op-

position and adversity. Amidst all the chaos, like a lot of us, I became

accustomed to quick fixes and, jumping the starting gun. Eventually I

overcame a lot, and became a very enlightened, open minded, artistic

and a productive survivor. I think I'm lucky. Maybe, I made out like a

bandit. Most kids that get bullied a lot in their toddler, elementary

and teenage years, can surely end up career criminals. I pulled my-

self through it, and, managed to stay out from behind bars, and, I am making an attempt to fit my secret into these few pages.

If you have, been bullied, beat up repeatedly, abused and / or

abandoned, you will benefit from the several scenarios I am carefully

including in this dialog.

As we grow, most of us find ourselves faced with a feeling

of emptiness, a void, that, we are not sure, sometimes, with what,

or how to fill it. Some of us resort to alcohol, legal and street drugs,

or gambling etc. Some find peace & serenity in religion. Regardless

less of what road you take, I want you to be assured that John Lennon

was correct when he stated in one of his last songs: 'Watching the

Wheels go 'Round'-- "I tell them there's no problems, only solutions."

If I get nothing else across in this short book, it would

surely be my intention to help you except that our feelings of love and

hate are characteristic of the human being. I'm showing you, what I

need to learn the most. This is not a how-to manual, compiled with

lectures about right and wrong. I am simply sharing with you the examples of the many pitfalls I became victim to, how I climbed

out, and finally learned to appreciate my potential. You can rest

assured also, that I won't be imposing my philosophy, nor will I make

proclamations about the cosmos or the origin of mankind.

The story doesn't get quite as bad as Jurassic Park, but

you'll want to hold on to your butts anyway.

Contents

FOREWORD

It is impossible
to find words
to discribe what is necessary
to those who do not know
what horror means
horror
horror has a face
and you must make a friend of horror
horror and moral terror
are your friends
If they are not
they are enemies to be feared
They are truly enemies...

Quote by Marlon Brando
In the movie: 'Apocalypse Now'
Author Unknown

1

RELEASED

The windows began to fog up while I was thinking about the many colors of the home made blanket I was bundled up in. The back of

the 1950s' station wagon was cold, but, it wasn't long before my mother,

Olla, my sister, and another woman were jumping in and driving the

car. I don't remember anything about the trip through the Dakotas,

Minnesota and Montana in route to the great North West. The first

memory I have of that time was shortly after we had arrived in Northern

Washington. It's scary to think about how I could have turned out.

Thankfully, I don't remember much about the place I was just about to be dropped off at and fried. The same goes for the many other facilities

my sister, Beth, and I were placed in, during our childhood.

It's been in just recent years that Beth, finally came forth, with

what she had witnessed while we were in the children's home. She saw

abuse that I don't recall. I, also saw something that, to this day, remains

in my head clear as a bell.

Our Mother, drove us that week, from the hospital in Louisville,

Kentucky to a city in Washington to place us in a children's home there

in 1955. I had eaten too much corn on the cob and caught rheumatic

fever, somehow, at the same time. It's surprising I lived through that with

the technology back then. I had an emergency appendectomy, but, I was

released shortly after wards, before leaving Kentucky.

There were quite a few children's homes all over the U. S. in the

50s and the 60s. A lot of the homes were reformatories for misfit kids out of control that were a result of so many broken homes. Unfortu-

nately, to continue receiving contributions and donations they were com-

pelled to except kids that were simply rejected by single parents.

Most of the kids were juvenile delinquents, and man, I was re-

minded of that daily. These kids saw me as a punching bag, early on.

A lot of struggling adults with unwanted children were the

candidates to usually qualify to place so many children's in homes back

then. The poor kids were showing all sorts of angry and vengeful

emotions, and, the more the dorm supervisors tried to keep them in

check, the meaner they got. The result is, they would take out their

frustrations on the other kids, and little animals, when they were around.

Our Mother was also a victim of abuse herself. I found out, in

later years, that she had developed some serious insecurities that, of

course, caused her to feel inadequate and withdrawn. Not to mention her mother, who was a very negative person, that broke mom's spirit early

on. She was not having an easy time, and, we were surely not valued and

in plans, following a wonderful honeymoon of a cherished marriage.

Mom, who was originally from Kentucky, had a very dark side. I don't

blame her for changing her name, and she did finally come around, to

accepting a lot more common sense, the last few years of her very

rambling, unstable and confused life. Mom was around a lot of bitterness.

She had a few run ends with some, not so nice associates, and became a

religious, close minded, bible pounding zealot- not fun to be with at all.

She seemed to be naïve in most respects, but I found things, difficult to

define, back then. Things like, we are not all born with the same innate-

ability as everyone. Even more shocking is, the fact, that researchers, now

are guessing that, some children are influenced by knowledge outside of our realm of existence and comprehension. Topping things off, I realize

now, that, Bethy and I were not only, suffering suckatashes from a broken

home, but we, also, were probably born, with a shortage of good genes,

genes that get children in the drivers seat at an early age. I want to

emphasize now, how greatly this affected my ability to effectively deal

with bullies. I do mean to say, too, that not all kids are born with a lack of

of a higher IQ from a parent that is short on smarts. I will say though,

that I firmly believe that I was lacking in the department, and, the count

of innate ability. Obviously, our mother was too.

The terror that went on in my mothers family before she and her

sisters left home was, actually, down right shocking. I got a taste, of the

magnitude of that fury visiting my, aunt Betty, in Northern, California

on my way back from Oregon back in 1983. She sat me down one night and commenced to share what she had witnessed one day, while

spending some time with our mom.

Mom, had been dating a nice gentleman in Kentucky. Our aunt ex-

plained that she could never get over our mothers' reaction when her

date, evidently said something she didn't like. Betty said, she saw her

pick up a cat and throw it into the mans face. The cat was scared, and

scatched the hell out of this guys face and neck. That same night, she also

shared her experience about grandma, and *her* fury. She said she found a

guy at school she took a liking to, and went out on a date one night. This

was back in the day when it was a very special privilege, yet a vulnerable

encounter to date someone. Our grandmother, Lupe, was so wrapped up

in her tactics & old fashion ways with a disciplinary iron fist, that, she was

completely against the idea of her daughter's mingling with the opposite sex while living under her roof. Betty, was probably around nineteen

or twenty years old at the time. She went on that night to divulge what a

wonderful, wholesome and meaningful, short time, she had with the man

she was interested in. When she returned home, Lupe, knowing she

was out on a date, stood at the doorway waiting, with bad intention that

night. She beat her in the face with a switch. Betty, left reluctantly

that night, and did not return for 20 years.

The behavior and the hate that seemed to be a constant in my

mothers family, I thought, was uncalled for and nothing seemed to add up

to motives. I felt so bad for both, our aunt, and our mother. They were

both victims of scenario, after scenario in situations that drove them to

develop a very mean side. Mom went over the top, and became so with-

drawn, that, I believe it took the religion & the church to give her better

ammunition that, she seemed to need, at the time,

I was not surprised hearing about the outrage. I guess you

could say I was beginning to collect a list of eccentric behaviors that were

adding up to make me feel like, it's no wonder I was uncomfortable

with her as a child. She had a sweet side, like most people do, but we did

not see it much.

I thought I would briefly share the two above scenarios, getting

started here, to give you an idea of the hostility, violence and insecurities

we were being influenced by at such a young and vulnerable age. It was no

doubt, the beginning recipe, concoction for a perfect bully magnet

that this book is attempting to define, and, the reasons why.

I can say, with a whole lot of confidence, that, looking back, I

realize that I got picked on a lot, mostly because, of how I reacted to *the*

bully approach. I can assure you with a high degree of certainty, that I

could have dodged a lot of grief and pain if I would have known how to

react to bullies with a more positive light.

Little did I know back when I was at the tender age of two, I would

begin to grow up so fast and witness things back then, that I would not

wish on my worst enemy. It all began there at that place in northern,

Washington not long after my sister saw kids beating me over the head.

Several mornings I would be forced to eat cold oats until I would throw

up, for, which, after wards, being severely punished. Nothing compared

with, nor was I, anywhere near ready, or prepared, to understand, or

decipher what happened one night, after we were there a while.

I slept in a baby crib in the corner of the large dormitory room

there upstairs of the children's home. I don't remember much about any-

thing else except that I was obviously awake and becoming uneasy. I do

remember the large room was like a military barracks. The other beds

were all lined up in formation next to each other with a center walkway.

The other boys were all fast asleep with little noise in the room. I saw

something in the center isle I thought was, out of the usual for that area

of the room. The rails of my baby bed were up, of course, and, I couldn't

fall, or get out. Hell, I was two years old, for Christs' sake, and, I never

had heard of, nor had any knowledge of the life after life.

    I heard a noise coming from that walkway. A trap door on the

floor opened up. There was light emitting out when, an odd old man

stepped out on to the floor as if he had climbed a latter from beneath

the hole he was climbing out. Rising to his feet quickly, he suddenly

begins to run down the walkway in my direction making a very loud

noise. It sounded like he had very hard heeled shoes, accompanied by

steel taps. He, then, begins to turn and charge toward my bed and simply

stops in front of me and stands there and stares. He had a blank look on his face as if to say "I know I'm scaring the be-Jesus out of you, but, this is

not my intention. I'm just out here looking around."

By this time I was literally choking from fear. I could not scream.

I couldn't talk, move, roll over or breath. I was simply horrified beyond

recovery. Every part of my body was in complete confusion with concrete

disbelief, as if I instinctively and intuitively knew, that, what I was seeing,

was not inside this realm of existence.

I remember looking over to my left and saw the dorm supervisor.

This woman was an exception to the cruelty that was so predominant

there in that place. I really cherish the memory of her suddenly

turning her head my way as she walked out into the hall. I recall thinking

that, wow, she sees it too. She has to! She is running now, toward my

baby crib, jerking me out and, running back toward her room. She

slams the door and places me on her bed. From that point on, I continued to see the apparition. I was pointing it out, but she did not see the

old man again. I remember the only way I could shut it off was to close

my eyes. I did the best I could to forget about it. I felt safe from it in her

room, and, the incident finally came to a rest.

   To this day the hair all over my body stands up every time I think

about that encounter. It is probably because the memory is so clear

and detailed. I've heard others say that when you see something like that,

it really stands out like nothing else. It's like you are recalling the ex-

perience in high definition. In my case, this happened sixty years ago,

and, I still can see those images like it happened last week.

   It wasn't long after that, our mother, came back and took us out

of that place. There were so few laws that protected children back then.

My sister and I, did have some weird experiences there. It was just the

beginning though, of a long rocky road for both of us.

Mom had mixed emotions when it came down to the question

of whether she really desired having us around full time. As the years

rolled by, it became obvious that she just was not capable of taking on the

responsibility of two kids. She did have a love / hate for us. I be-

lieve that, if she had the financial and emotional support of a spouse

member, she could have pulled it off better than she did, but, she is

the one that chose to grab us and split. At least that was her story, but,

to this day, we are both skeptical about what exactly went on between

her and our legal father. She claimed he was abusive and she left him.

I think there were actually quite a few missing lines, blanks and holes in

that story. Never-the-less, the sister and I developed an awareness and

the ability to read people. You could say that this kept us in check and out

of trouble, on the most part, in spite of the many predators and bullies that constantly plagued our childhood. With that kind of chaos, and,

instability at such a young age, we began to embrace the dark side of

people, places and things. We had no choice but to make a friend of the

evil and hate we were surrounded with. Thus, we began to learn to

tolerate the darkness so we could consume the light when it offered itself

as a retreat.

I really can't remember where, exactly, we lived after Mom came

and took us out of that children's home. I do recall being in El Paso, Texas

at six years old at a beautiful college, and, falling in love with a girl

three times my age who was in school there. She was a looker, and, she

had the same crush on me in spite of our age difference. I did have

fond memories of the school yard and the students there.

Mom, did have a teaching certificate. She was teaching mostly

English along with special reading courses to kids that needed extra help getting started. I recall the children spoke favorably about our mother &

her methods. I was to find out later that she was bringing too much

gospel and religious material into the class that was just as illegal back

then as it is now. The difference was, that, this was a Christian school, so,

to some degree she was on the right page with what she was supposed to

teach there.

    I remember jumping off a fence and breaking my arm. Mom, sure

seemed to think it was just a spring and never took me to the doctor.

My arm healed wrong, but... I have always been able to play guitar.

    Mom, found another children's home in Texas when I was close to

my 8th birthday. It wasn't nearly as hard to get along there. The dorm

supervisors were nice and not such over-kill disciplinarians. For once,

my young roommate wasn't the equivalent of an ex-con, on cell block nine.

Instead he actually had a sense of humor and made me laugh a lot. Thus

proving that not all the children's homes back then were totally un-

desirable. Which brings me now to talk about the third home our mom

placed us in. This time, though, it was a boys ranch. She seemed to be so

naive about the intent and reasons for these establishments. 'Wiley Boys

Ranch' was definitely a court ordered alternative haven for boy teens

that had been in serious trouble with violent crimes and drug possession.

Each time she would find these places, usually at a church, and de-

cide to try another alternative, she never seemed to consider the fact,

that, I had never been in trouble with the law.

I was still just eight when she talked me in to agreeing to try,

this ranch, sixty miles East of Dallas, Texas. I have to tell you, this

was some kind of umbrella. Several shocking events and experiences

took place there, all within a three month period.

The ranch was well organized. There were several dorms in the

shape of a home that had several bedrooms with their own kitchen and

living space. I had no idea just how mean the dorm supervisor was until

working with him outside. We were installing a plumbing overflow pipe

one day, I was working, trying to help fill in dirt and cover it up after we

laid it in a trench. It had been raining. The supervisor, was on his knees

working with his hands on something. I accidentally got too much dirt on

my shovel and splashed a little muddy water on his arm. He immediately

picked up a whole hand full of mud and threw it into my face. I, right

away, became humiliated. I withdrew and was too shaken & embarrassed

to wipe off the mud and forget it happened. It was as if, I felt like, I was

supposed to wear the mud for the rest of the day- A perfect example of a child raised without direction on how to deal with someone who simply

thinks we all needed to be punished. He would show this kind of aggres-

sion at every event, and, each related moment. The supervisor, Mr. Lee,

was real big, tall and strong. The man just didn't like us-not a

good match for someone whom we were supposed to learn from.

I was soon to find he was not the only man there with an appe-

tite for causing extreme discomfort. The ranch was surrounded with

activities and equipment to give the boys a recreational outlet in the

afternoons after we all were given morning chores. It all worked well.

I gotta hand it to the person who organized all that, because, I had

the time of my life with those activities. They had trampolines, volleyball,

horse shoes, basketball, tennis, football, baseball, horseback riding, hiking

and swimming.

I remember electing swimming one day. I had got my suit on

and, was sitting on the edge of the pool alongside of the other boys that

day. One of the kids got to horsing around a little and pushed me into the

pool. The, so called, coach of the activity that afternoon, told us to get out

and follow him into his office. He then commences to get out a paddle

made from a baseball bat and told me to bend over. The guy beats me

hard with several hard aggressive hits. He beats the other kid with the

same kind of attack. The beating was so severe, I had a back ache, all that

week. The man claimed we were misbehaving, but, what is so hard

for me to believe is that I was not holding any animosity toward anyone

those early days. It was as if I had very little dignity and the ability to

recognize I needed help with people walking all over me.

I was being crucified. I had quit trying to get ole J.C. to help me out.

There were a lot of mean kids there at the ranch, but, there were several boys who really liked me. We really valued the unity we had

going on for the most part. I elected horse back riding several times. I ac-

tually became attached to a horse named 'Nelly'. Is that a typical name

for a horse or what? Anyhow, after riding the horses on several different

occasions, Mr. Lee decided to ride with us one day. I was on Nelly while

a friend was on another horse. I was so young and new to riding that I lost

control that day when the two horses decided to take off and run. Horses

naturally like to sprint every chance they get if they are healthy, and it

is, of course, up to the rider to keep the animal in control. I tried but

could not stop Nelly. The two ran about a half a mile down a dirt road.

We gained control and came on back to where Mr. Lee planted himself.

He immediately tells us to get off and run the distance that the horses ran. Again, these supervisors, had the typical notion that children should

always be within the guidelines of what the supervisors had dreamed up

to be kosher. So it boiled down to the guidelines being invented by the

guardians as they went along. Obviously, these disciplinarians were

not answering to anybody who thought they needed to be monitored.

You could be a violent ruthless cowboy in the sixties. Law Enforcement

back then was very different. There were hundreds of unsolved murders

and mutilations. Which now brings forth the shocking story I was then to

witness, shortly after the fun I had with Mr. Lee and the horses.

I had just met two great teens, shortly after I settled in there

at the dorm. Billy was in a room next to mine, and Rudy was also, close,

just down the hall. They both liked me. I seemed to see things the same

way they both did. We laughed and joked together.

One day Billy came into my room and said as he exposed his butt "look what Mr. Lee did to me." My jaw dropped when I saw

that he had been beaten with a board so hard that his flesh looked like

hamburger meat. He was still bleeding hours after he had been attacked

by the so called dorm supervisor. It was hard to believe what I was seeing,

but, I did believe it, because, it kept happening to me. I remember

thinking that this can't be right. I thought, that, a higher up needs to

know about all this overkill of the so-called discipline.

Rudy came into my room the next day to ask if he could borrow

my canteen. He claimed he and Billy were choosing to engage the hiking

activity for that afternoon. I had a World War Two TA-50 belt with a light

weight aluminum container for water, that, I got somewhere. I really

valued the whole belt. It was the one thing I had that I really cherished.

I did notice the two, packing in a bunch of can goods, beef jerky and other things to eat. I thought it to be a bit odd, that, they would be packing food

to that extent just for an afternoon walk, but, I said yes. They filled up the

canteen and were soon taking off for the hike. Two days later, we were

to find out some shocking news about what those two had up their sleeve.

The news was really hard to swallow, and, all of us who knew the

two precious teens, became very sad when the truth arrived about them.

They kept going, ran away, hit the road. They split the whole program.

The breaking news was: "Two boys walked on to a farmers property, stole

the mans rifle, threatened the wife & took off with their ranch pick-up."

I had no idea, just how distraught, both of them really were.

Even if I did and had the compassion to care enough to try to help in some

way, who would I have been able to confront? The supervisors were such

a bunch of Nazis' that counseling was not an option.

They got on the two lane road heading to town going too fast,

of course. A cop spotted the pick-up right away, and, began a chase. I

assume the two sped up adding fuel to the situation. We were told they

eventually had a team of police after them. They ended up in a shoot

out with several cops. It was unthinkable for those days. We're talking the

sixties' here! Sadly, Billy, was shot to death. Rudy, lived after

being shot in the shoulder and ended up with a long sentence in a Texas

prison. I heard later, that, Rudy had been beaten several times by Lee.

I was devastated. At that point, it was all down hill for me. I was be-

coming extremely depressed. I declined to attend the funeral for

Billy.

Olla, must have picked up my signal, because, it wasn't long after

that, that she traveled there to visit. We went for a ride to one of the lakes

near by. I tried to tell her about all that had taken place, in the 3 months without sobbing. I couldn't even talk. She thought I was making

it all up until we collaborated some of the incidents with a couple of the

other boys who had even more horror stories to tell, to boot!

This time I was really at the mercy of my mother, who was not

being very understanding at the time. She knew the place was over-

kill for boys who were there, simply because their parent claimed they

could not support them. Thankfully, she finally came out that day and

told the officials there at the ranch, after hearing the news...

"You know, I think I'll take him."

I'll never forget those words. We went back to my dorm, packed my

things, and, I was released.

2

LOVING IN EL PASO

Nobody deserves to be criticized, and, really, few of us surpass

good enough. We just pull it off, get through it, and manage it all, loving

it or hating it. Every one of us should be given the credit, and, a pat on

the back if we have survived into our 30s without taking ourselves out, or

getting arrested for murder on the job front.

I never did hold any animosity toward our mother. She acted ac-

cordingly, and, did what she knew to be the best for Beth and me, as well

as, for herself. I have learned not to hold a grudge. It is so much more important to put yourself in the shoes of others, before you judge hard,

even when people let you down. I just never had it in me, to become en-

tirely, unforgiving.

Our Mother, hung around a few people in California who, from

what I hear, could have been involved with the Mob. She seemed to

be very ashamed to talk about her past, to us, before she hooked up with

our dad. She did say she drank alcohol and smoked at parties, but she was

involved in a very bad automobile accident and was thrown from the car.

Mom, would talk about pain she had, in her neck and back. She began

having migraine headaches at an early age, to boot. With that combi-

nation of tragedy and inherited ailments, Mom, turned to religion and

caught, what some people call, the 'Christian disease'. She became over

kill in that capacity, to the point of repelling some folks, and, that would surely include Beth and me. That's not to mention the nagging voice

she had. It was the kind of obnoxious approach that radiated a pestilence

when entering a room. I tried to overlook these attributes about mom. I

continued to feel so incompatible. When she would do some research and

find a boys ranch, or another children's home, I remember pleading

with her to take me back to, a ranch or, anywhere, but there with her.

She did want to love and except us, but, she needed something like

Christianity to put a label on her methods. She needed a signature label

to be an acceptable disciplinarian, and, a qualified single parent. Bless her

heart. She was so insecure. We could hardly reason with her. It was im-

possible to be her friend. She was constantly allowing the religious

dogma, fundamentalism to keep a wedge driven between her and us kids.

There was little knowledge of alternative steps, back then, when it came down to getting through to children concerning mother / child

reunion. Olla was a mess. I was growing up to be a pretty dumb kid

the more I stayed with her in-between moving from town to town. She

kept telling us there's no reason to improve your house. Jesus is coming

for us all next week. Fortunately, Beth and I were not buying that idea.

It could have been because she used the bible and the fundamentalism

as a weapon in her approach. It all came out like a threat. If we would

disagree or rebel in any way, she, would hammer us with scare tactics.

We both were just sick to death of all those years of chastisement that

degraded both of us to the point of thinking she was some kind of witch.

It has all begun to make sense now. Just this year, when applying

for a new job, I had to get an extensive DOT physical, and, the company

required a psychoanalysis. For the first time in my life, I got to talk to a psychiatrist. After mapping out my childhood and attempting to de-

fine my mothers' insecurity and unsettled behavior, he put me at ease.

Suddenly everything began to make sense. What he said was, "She

probably had a mental illness."

Texas, is one place, of which, I must say, I have many fond

memories. I recall, so vividly, watching John F. Kennedy's funeral on a

nineteen sixty two television. I was in the third grade on La Luz street

there. I had two girlfriends at the same time, and, I was able to turn

Olla off pretty often those days. She kept moving from house to house

there in Texas. We must have lived in four rentals while I was in grade

school.

One day, out of the blue, she decided to go visit her mother in

Louisville, Kentucky. This was our fist trip back there since I was in the

Kentucky hospital when I was two. I can't say enough, now, just how awesome it was to experience Kentucky. I was born there, but don't re-

member anything about it. Driving in, late at night, beholding the

cool summer air and witnessing the magic luminous of the fire flies

was such an unforgettable trip, for the curious child that I was, and still

am.

I got to meet our grandmother for the first time on that journey.

She seemed very friendly and accommodating in her sixties, but, I found

the next 3 visits we made back there, kinda odd. These visits would re-

veal some things about our family history. My moms' dad was a well liked,

a hard working, compassionate, nice guy. He died young. I never met him,

but, I heard he was a tough act to follow. My grandmother, Lupe Franco

remarried a man named 'Mark'. It appeared, she became, kind of bitter

after becoming an instant caregiver for him as he became quite ill in his golden years... We did visit her again when she was caring for him. It

became obvious to me, at that time, that, Lupe showed a very dark side.

I saw a lot a negativity in her mannerism that obviously spilled over on to

Olla's approach. I began to understand why Olla became so mean

and critical of us, and, I certainly understand now how tough it was for

both Lupe and Olla having so much responsibility. Neither of them got

much help, from any other family members. Olla never stuck around at

any one place long enough to make decent friends & to build any kind of a

solid social foundation. This was a terrible influence on us kids.

It seems like it was our second trip back there that our moms'

car threw a rod in the engine-to top off her luck. I remember having to

ditch the car and take a bus to Kentucky. I was so glad we did get

there because I found out something about our grandmother that turned

out to be a tremendous advantage. I was to discover that she was a 'white witch'. Olla said, Lupe, could naturally remove the warts I had all over

my hands. Our grandmother really shocked me when she, in deed, man-

aged to pull it off. She would take a piece of straw from, who knows,

where, then, while breaking it over the wart, she would recite a parable,

or some kind of mysterious phrase. Then, lo and behold, one to two weeks

later, the wart, no matter the size, would simply vanish in a very short

time. I mean, I would wake up one morning, and, it would be gone. This

really helped me to overlook the extreme negative personality that our

grandmother had. I sure developed a value for her. I couldn't

help but fit in a lot of respect and love for her, as hard as it was, to be a-

round her.

We visited Lupe about every three years while we were growing

up and moving from house to house, city to city and state to state. We ended up moving to a small village called La Homa. It was just twenty

five miles north of Santiago, NM. We must have been there every bit

of a month when mom decided to move again. She'd seek greener grass in

the next town. I remember her always forcing us to go to church when we

kept trying to get out of it. People in the churches' would always say:

"My God Olla, the Lord has work for you, but, it probably is not here in

this town. God has a mission for you. More than likely, it would be in

a larger, or different town." She would consider all this, to be prophecy.

She would take this stuff to heart, and, yank up roots all of a sudden. We

would meet and make friends at school. Then, the next month, we would

move again.

They say that a parent has much more of an impact on your life

than you might imagine. This idea has surely made a lot of sense to me lately. After leaving home at age fifteen, I did mostly the same thing-

move, then move, then move again. I was uncomfortable to remain any-

where for very long.

I have to admit though, I really enjoyed visiting grandmother in

Louisville, especially after finding her to be a mysterious person, and, a

white witch. The warts did not come back. It would seem that the spell

that she cast got rid of the wart virus, to boot. She also had a very green

thumb. The tomatoes she raised in her back yard were to die for. I will al-

ways treasure the memories of being in her back yard. The greenery and

inevitable plush grass and vegetation was like a dream.

Grandmother had a mean side though. To give you an idea of

just how bad, my aunt Betty, in California, told me another shocking

tale. After hearing about her episode with Lupe, I began to see why our

mother had the split personality and such a mean streak. To be raised by a parent that thought it was necessary to strike out at a child on a daily

basis was, seemingly typical. It was after we moved from La Homa, New

Mexico that, Olla started slugging me in the face. I was loosing respect for

our mother. I felt like I could not trust her to be there for me as a friend.

She was, as much over kill with her so-called discipline, as she was in her

religious belief. I was growing up to be a really scarred, ignorant and

pathetic outcast. I just wasn't learning any coping skills, nor any survival

values. In short, I was a mess. It seems to me now, that, if I learned

anything worth keeping in my soul and brain back then, it was because

I was mostly raised in the boys ranches and children's homes. Places

where, there, were at least, other kids who were going through similar

circumstances. I was too young to even know pity. I didn't even know how

to feel sorry for myself. It didn't even occur to me that I was being mistreated and abused. I was brand new to life. I figured this was all normal

and the way life was for every one. To some degree, it WAS the norm

to be poor as dirt and come from a broken home. I had no reason to think

there was a better way. I saw other families that were even worse off.

I was getting to be around nine years old when we then moved

from Madero to Mohave, New Mexico. Beth, and I lived with Olla

for a longer time this go around. I loved El Paso a lot, and, I wished

we never left there. I did everything from, run away from home there to,

being introduced to the Beatles. I will never forget where I was standing

on Manson avenue when one of my little neighbor friends was saying

something about them. I thought he meant there was some kind of odd

bug in his yard. He took me inside, and he played, "I want to hold your

hand," on a turntable. I was so impressed. I grew to love the Beatles.

We had been building scooters to ride down our neighborhood

sidewalk. Manson ave was ending into a mountain. We were on quite a

hill. My young friends across the street came up with the idea of using

their roller skates, and, hooking them on a long board front and back. We

had an instant go-cart, that, would go very fast, being on such a fantastic

steep hill. We simply had the time of our lives those short lived days.

This was also the time that us kids were getting up to the ridge of the

mountain so close to our block. Builders had taken some equipment there

and cut into a hill creating a cliff around forty feet high. I was very leery

about this formation. I seemed to have a little common sense at a young

age. I stayed off the top of that rock mainly because the hill slanted

so much. I just knew someone would eventually get nutty and have an

accident of some kind there, and, I was right. Lo and behold, a few weeks later, kids we didn't know, were playing up there. One of them fell off.

He broke his leg in three places and had to be rescued. There were cops

and firemen all over that place. It made the six-o-clock news, and, we just

about got into the picture. I'll never forget how scary that was watching

them carry the poor kid down that mountain with him being in agonizing

pain. To say the least we were horrified around that place in many res-

pects. Just a few days later when we went back up there I ran into a rattle

snake that was sunning itself out in the open. It spooked when we dis-

turbed it, and quickly crawled back under the rock. I must say, I surely

began to feel very safe, OFF, of that mountain, cozy in my little bed room

loving life in Texas.

Olla, met a man at the school in the early 60s. He became sort

of a mentor for our ridiculous little family. He was the minister there of a Pentecostal church while we were in Texas. I think mom knew him

before Beth was born. His name was Robert Crump. He had a wife that

I grew to find one of the sweetest people I had ever met up to that

point in my life, and, her name was Kita. Our mother seemed to have

latched on to this couple for dear life. He was so eager to help us, but,

Olla took advantage. She would let him help her with her needs. Then

she would turn around and blame him for getting her in to a situation

that she claimed was not of Gods' direction or will. This was not good

influence for us kids, but, I surely felt a lot a love coming from this couple.

   We ended up calling them uncle Robbie and aunt Kita. They were up

in their years and were already having ailments trying to get the best of

them. I will always cherish sitting on a couch in their apartment

with aunt Kita. She sat there one day stroking the back of my head in the most loving way. I will never forget the depth of the love I felt while

sitting with her that day. There are moments in our lives that have such

a profound effect on us, that it is hard to find words to describe these

feelings. I must say, that, this was one of those times. The uncon-

ditional caring I felt from this person healed a lot of scars that I had

collected up to that point. These two people were precious beyond words,

and, what is ironic, is, that, they were both in their eighties. They con-

tinued to monitor us for quite a while there in Texas, as old as they were.

Mr. Crump died from emphysema, five years, after moving from El Paso.

We moved again across town shortly after the Kennedy assassina-

tion. Olla found a place next to a flood control reservoir wash. The river

area was dry if it wasn't raining- a lot like the river beds in Arizona. There

were two large pipes that fed into a very large concrete control house.

You could get to the housing through both pipes that joined parallel.

It was a young boys paradise playground! The little friends I met soon

after we moved there, enjoyed the fascination as well as I did. We all

would go down there and hang out in that room. It would seem that I had

begun to develop a radar sense of suspecting danger in other children

by the initial noises they would bellow those days. Sure enough, we

were in the control flood house one day when we heard another group

of kids entering one of the pipes. They were approaching the area where

we were in the south pipe. A voice was ringing in my good judgment ear.

I, right away, began to warn the other boys that we need to split before

they get here, and, I was right. I said we need to wait until they get a-

bout three quarters of the way here. We are then, going to make a mad

dash through the other pipe, and get out! Sure enough, we pulled it off.

Those kids, turned out to be the meanest and most threatening bullies in

the school we all went to. The boys, I was hanging with, could not believe

how sure footed I had been that day making the decision to guide us out.

We stood there on the river bank and tried to talk to these guys after

we tricked them, escaping. They started throwing rocks aggressively.

I went on home, and I realized these nut cases would surely be after us

from that point on. Olla decided to move again. This time, our

mothers' rambling behavior, and, tendency to move so often, served as a

tremendous advantage. Just before we moved, I found myself having

to walk home alone after seeing Boris Carlofs' original 'Frankenstein.'

It was the 1st horror movie I had ever seen. It really had me trembling

in my shoes that night. It was probably scarier than having that reservoir

bully after me. I found the movie so fascinating that, I begged Olla, who drove to the friends house where I was, to please, let me stay to finish

seeing it to the end. Again, I was quickly learning, and, I found myself

attracted to fear that I felt compelled to overcome. Olla, was **NOT**

coming to my aide in supplying me with tactics on how to approach and

deal with the bullies that were constantly attacking me. To see a

monster like Frankenstein being chased and hunted down like an animal,

I must say, was definitely something I needed to see til the end. It was

typical of our mother who wouldn't wait fifteen minutes. She drove on

home that night leaving me to walk back two miles in the dark. All I could

see was Frankenstein around every corner, hiding in every bush waiting

to devour my scared little body. I was a mess that night, but, I lived on

to become open, always curious about, and a fan of good horror.

We must have lived on Mansan avenue up the street to the West for over a year-a long time, for our pathetic, lost little nomadic family. I

just loved that block, and, I found, looking back, that I was loving all of

the places we lived there in El Paso. I was ten years old going on twenty.

By that time I had been subjected to so many changes and challenging

scenarios that my head was spinning. The perfect life, for a child, to end

up desperate for stress relief. I would later find, that, I was not going

to find it in, nor obtain it from our mother. We had actually begun to

plant some roots in that city. Olla, became influenced by someone else at

the church we were going to. She pulled up roots again. Uncle Robby

moved to Santiago, and, after living in El Paso, for a five or six years,

we, also moved to Santiago. I'll never forget, all of the unusually great

memories, along with the depth of closeness to the little friends I had on that block. Just before we left though, our neighbors tried to fix the wife.

I developed a tremendous appreciation for the kids next door to us, and,

I surely need to briefly share the things I experienced meeting that family

there. Lina and Lisa were my age, but, their mother had multiple sclero-

sis. The poor lady spent all of her days on the living room floor so she

could crawl from there to other rooms for her needs. The two kids were

in school all day, of course, and the dad was also away at work, every day,

as well. Those days it must have been tough to get any home care funding

or caregivers willing to stay there with her all day. I suppose, with enough

money one could have even got an RN to stay with her. Needless to

say, they didn't have a lot. It seems he worked in a store somewhere.

I went over for a visit one day to find they had all left town. A

neighbor said the family had gone to an Evangelistic convention/ revival in Florida. The husband had been influenced to believe that this evan-

gelist was, with no doubt, going to immediately, heal his wife, as if he had

a magic wand. They returned after a few days. I found her back down

on the floor, after hurrying over for a visit, hoping to find her walking

around. Even at the age of nine, I was skeptical. Sure enough, the

family came back frantically disappointed. As young as I was, I felt very

badly for them. They had traveled that distance with no help, really, from

anyone. They must have been devastated. I loved those two precious

little girls. The mother was a very sweet person, that, was trapped in

a very immobile body. You can only imagine what that did to their faith.

There were evangelists on television all the time those days using stunts

to act out being blind or lame and magically cured in a matter of a few

seconds. I find it hard to believe that there are still people abroad, and, in the U.S. that continue to hand out their hard earned cash to these nutty

television evangelists'. Us kids were all so young, but, we were wit-

nessing alot of extremes those days, and, it was mostly because we kept

moving, then, moving again...

I thought, I would place special importance and emphasis on the

early years of my childhood. To be brief as possible, I've always been one

of those guys that likes to get right to the point. I don't want to be too

over-kill with harping on the misfortune of being raised having such

difficulty. To put things in the light of what I'm trying to communicate, it

is important that we all understand, why I became a bully magnet. Above

all else, I'll never point the finger at our mother, her family, my father or

any kin. Family stability, requires the entire recipe. The absence of

that solid foundation, from the get-go, is what drives a child to reach for love & acceptance most anywhere possible. Like most kids, I didn't think

there was anything wrong! My self esteem was in trouble. I had very few

productive values. We were without goals and dreams, we had no aim.

The more we moved around, the less I engaged in activities that promoted

going into a productive direction. My aura spelled, a big 'LOST,' so guess

what? To top things off, bullies easily spotted me. My face, must

have looked, to them, like a big target painted on a sitting duck. At this

point, the main attribute, that was missing, was communication skills. If a

child does not have an adult around to give 'em some pointers, where is

that kid going to learn to rationalize and make any solid, sane decisions?

I'll tell you where! I firmly believe that, if we would have done one thing

right, when Beth and I, were growing up, it would be to stay in one place-

one town, one state, one house, one home. If we would have done that, over half of our problems with these monsters would never have even

gotten started. If I were to give any advice at the starting gun, it would

surely be, to "stay settled down." At least until kids graduate from high

school.

There was a couple of reasons our Olla decided to leave El Paso.

I didn't know it at the time, but this move would prove to be, one of our

most challenging fly by night ideas. I hadn't really come into serious con-

tact with a lot of cruelty up to that point. The kids I knew, and had such

fun with, on that block were probably the best times of my childhood.

I was full of creative energy, and, excited about our home, and, loved the

school. We had a wonderful landscape that drew a lot of fun people. The

two boys across the street were always keeping me on my toes with

interesting sporty games to play. Lina and Lisa, were fun, even though their mom was ill. We had a great back yard with grass and vege-

tation. Our mother would beat us a lot with her paddle, but, I was not so

affected to depress me. I liked our house. I liked the desert. I loved Robby

and Kita. I did OK in school. I found out about the Beatles on that block. I

just simply, totally, and, whole heartedly found myself, loving in El Paso.

3

BULLIES IN SANTIAGO

Growing up in a bunch of small towns in the Wild, Wild West did

not serve as any kind of advantage for kids in the 60s. The reasons we

moved again to another little city, was nonsense. We were too scattered.

Our mother was just, too confused, about purpose. She thought she

was practicing a purpose, but she lacked the entrepreneurial skills and

ideas to target and execute a solid subject. I don't think she believed she

deserved to make good money. Therefore, she never did see the need to

network with people with a common goal. Unfortunately, if a person did not start out being influenced by the parent, especially those days, one

would have surely needed to go to a college that taught business and sales

skills. It's a whacky world now though. Yep, if you did not get started on

a, reel-'em-in-venture, such as: find, develop, fund, market and patent a

product or idea, you could miss that train. I missed the train. You do

learn a lot when that happens. I started out so full of excitement and

creative energy. Now I am going to begin to relate to you what happens

when a dog gets beat too much. It's a train, I will show you how to exit.

I've heard it said, when I've been in conversations with people

talking about depression, that you can break kids spirit when you

insist on calling 'em a moron, or, you continue to not give him / her the

benefit of a doubt. I think this is one of the reasons I developed a lot of

horse sense early on. I always have felt some what confident and sure footed in practical decision making. Believe me, this did not happen

over night. It became a focus point for me, because, I had developed so

many insecurities, and, like Olla, I felt unaccepted and inferior around a

lot of people. If you get nothing else out of this book, remember this

one thing. "A lot of successful people will do their darndest to make you

feel like you are someone they won't respect." This has always been!

My poor mother would meet people at the church, of all places, come

home and worry that they did not like, or, except her. To some extent,

I have suffered these tendencies myself. It has taken years to over

come. Like I said, I can't emphasize enough, about how important it is, to

know, just how much of an impact our parents have on us.

We moved in to a large brick house in Santiago, N.M. that was

built, probably before the high school, across the street. It is a three bed room, with a large porch. It was great to have my own room after

we tried living a short time in another children's home in Northern

Arkansas. We were only there a few weeks. It wasn't a bad place. I re-

member not having much privacy, but, I began to adjust to the move

quite readily. I was in third grade, and I attended the the elementary

state school, two blocks away in Santiago, after leaving Arkansas.

Without realizing it, up to this point, I was soon to find out that I

had been groomed to be another bully magnet-with all the ingredients

to concoct the precise idiot formula. When it came down to self esteem

and standing up for myself, I was a mess. I just wasn't prepared for what

I was just about to be confronted with. I needed some help, and I was still

not getting any, from adults at school, nor at home.

The one bully scenario that really sticks out was, when I was confronted by a big fat boy who picked me out, and, of course, I didn't have

the foggiest idea of why he would target me. Kids were always, picking a

fight with me. Not knowing what to say or how to react, I would agree to

to meet them somewhere after school when that was the last thing I

meant to say. It was like I said it to satisfy their need to be all powerful, by

allowing the guy to be better than me. Is that stupid or what? Absolutely

God damned right that's stupid! Now, maybe you can see what kind of

influence I was getting from Olla. The impact of a parent was so strong.

Oh, Man, what I would give to turn back the hand of time. Regret? Nope.

Just fantasizing about handling all that stuff very differently if given a

second chance. Wars get started from misunderstandings and communi-

cation break down. It's important to be prepared; always. We can never be too prepared. You learn these things well in martial arts, and, I am going

to discuss a little bit about that, in chapters ahead.

I don't remember this fat boys name. He stuck out like a sore

thumb. He saw me that day as an easy push over. He starts pushing me

down repeatedly while on lookers stood, there, entertained. I must have

been half his size. He wasn't going to cut me a break. After hitting the

asphalt several times I figured I stood little chance. I got up sobbing and

fled hoping he was not following me. All I needed to do was pick up some

dirt (I remember we were kicking around in plenty) and blind the fat boy

landing a good swift kick breaking his nose. I was finding out nicely

how little I knew about defending myself. I managed to get away with just

some minor cuts and scrapes. He never did completely stop picking on

me, but, he mostly came at me with verbal harmful intent after that first day. Unacceptable! You just don't let someone do you that way. First of all

he had no reason to antagonize me. Second place, I should never have

agreed to meet him somewhere after school to duke it out. Thirdly,

I should have questioned him about his motive. If you simply attempt to

reason with a bully, you are at least relating to them to perhaps divert

their attention long enough to express the idea that maybe you might

share something in common. "We could possibly find something else

to do this afternoon." If you relate to people, with these kind of inse-

curities that you know something better than using your muscle brain,

sometimes they will listen. People are hungry. Most people will

stop and think "wow maybe we could do something else tonight that just

might be more fun and rewarding." I think I could have done both. Throw

dirt in his eyes and still got through to him...The trick: "Out smart 'em!"

I really loved the big house we rented. It had 3 bed rooms. It was

a wonderful red brick home. It still stands today. We had a young dog

there. I named him Sammy. That poor dog, like a lot of children, I

took out some of my frustrations on him. Being a dog that was getting

beat too much myself was surely not good for a child/dog reunion.

Olla began, at this point, to beat me more and more with a board over

every little thing. She started jabbing my hand with a fork at the

table for reaching for something that she deemed, taboo. According

to her, most everything outside the church was, taboo. Going to a movie

was a sin. Drinking wine was a sin. Looking at girls, reading horror, going

to movies and wearing short skirts, was all taboo. This drove Beth nuts.

What made me most uncomfortable, was, that Olla insisted that

we take the bible literally and forced us, to go to church. She would turn

around and slap or slug me in the face for the slightest acts of opposition or rebellion of any degree. I ran away one time when we were in El Paso.

When the cops found me, and, I returned, she beat me extremely hard

not even realizing that, that was the reason I split in the first place.

I don't think it ever crossed her mind how severely she was com-

pletely 'watering down my spirit'. Hang on to those words. You can't cut a

child in half and give 'em a band-aide. I was nine years old. I was being

harassed and beat up at school then coming home to a parent, beating me

to boot. Great googlely mooglely! You gotta *praise* a kid once in a while.

I guess you could say this was the most challenging phase of

my confusion and dealings with new confrontations of violence. My child-

hood artistic excitement was going south for me. I was loosing it. I think

the thing that saved me, was meeting Mario, who lived on the corner

of 3rd and Pinonalita. We really appreciated each other. The great fun we had making forts, digging holes and camping out in the ground,

looking back, really made a statement. The image of myself, that I was

beginning to develop, was starting to look and feel like, I was born in a

toilet and, raised in a cesspool.

Mario, was my age, and we had some great times together. I just

loved that kid. Saturdays, we would literally do anything to manage to

get together. He had two brothers. The mother and dad got along well. So

I found that family to be good medicine, and I felt, loved, there. They

took away a lot of the anxiety I was having there at such a young age.

A few weeks later, I was at the school play ground on a weekend

alone. I loved to spend time on the swing sets and use the tether ball. A

couple of Hispanic kids walked up and greeted me there and acted

normally. They sat down joining me on a swing but began to yell for a third boy to come down to the school play area. They proceeded to

scream until their friend finally got there. I was soon to find that all along

the three had been premeditating to execute an attack on me and spent a

good two hours terrorizing me with sticks, rocks, threats and doing some

harm, tripping me on to the gravel. I think I bled in several places.

The thing that bothers me most to this day, is the fact that they waited til

there was at least three of them, and persisted to gang up as if to say they

felt like two of them may not be able to consume the helpless kid. That

was one of the first times I felt completely defenseless. I regret to say that

most Hispanic kids in my past would always be friendly to my face while

around public places during school, but one, would never approach me

with harmful intent by himself. It wasn't surprising. "Tough guys, don't

don't talk tough." Wars get started when people in power never grow up.

It becomes obvious that children are developing insecurities when they

pick on the weaker kid. What about now? You could almost say that

present day attacks are even worse. We have simply found more

sophisticated ways of beating each other over the head.

I survived the attacks, but I continued to be terrible at handling

confrontations. Three more Latin American kids ganged up on me a few

days later in front of the high school right across the street from our

house. One of them kept telling me to kiss his ass. Once again, if I

could only turn back the hand of time, when these kids kept terrorizing

me, I would have bit a chunk of meat out of that monkeys' seat!

Its' ironic when we look back at our child hood days. It doesn't

usually occur to us that this stuff was just not a very sane life style if you

were to compare it to children in England, for example. I have often

thought about how intelligent some of these kids are, that, were a part of the British invasion. The brilliance and quality of so many awesome songs

were so full of examples to live by and learn from. I have often wondered

how, where, why and what these kids were exposed to, and paid attention

to, arriving with so much creativity? Why in the U.S. would we would

have 2000 murders, for every three, in Great Britain. What is it over here?

Why so much violence here? This is our best question so far in this book.

If I try and define it, I believe it will simply appear to be one of a

million opinions. Survival has become complicated in the United States.

I was surely becoming familiar with opposition and adversaries at

face value in Santiago. It was one bully gang after another in the first

few months there, but, lo and behold, to my surprise, the day came that

I would first meet someone I would never forget.

I was at home, one warm summer day with Beth. A man out of

the blue was knocking at our front door. I did not hear the knock. Olla called both of us to the living room, and, sitting there was a long, skinny

legged, dark haired mysterious figure. He stood up. It looked like he was

going to collide with the ceiling. I took one look. For some odd reason

I knew it was my own sweet dad. I threw my arms around his legs shou-

ting, daddy. He had little to say. I, of course, don't remember just what,

exactly, he did say. This moment in time would sure prove one thing.

I found out that day just how crazy Olla was. I do remember him sugges-

ting that we all sit down at the table for tea. Mom made us all some lipton

tea she hardly ever drank her self, nor us either. She was a heavy coffee

consumer, but, we all sat there and talked about, nothing, I guess.

Nothing significant. I'm sure, I was drifting in my mind, about what in the

world he was up to. Shortly after a brief conversation, Olla started in on

him. She began to confront him with whatever his shortcomings were.

I remember her getting louder as she was becoming angry. Then talking

herself in to a fit of rage where she was practically spitting at him. He

gets up and moves toward the front door. She continues to spat at him

with the pettiest quarrel I had ever seen up to that day. She starts

slugging him on his chest, screaming violently, non stop. The poor man

looks at us and, simply says; "well, I guess I should be leaving now." We

were so used to changes at that point, that, it really didn't phase Beth

and me. It was the first time we ever saw our father. We had done with

out him for all that time, so, I figured this is what families do. This is how

it is. Is that dumb or what? There goes our dear ole dad. He gets in his

car and drives off into the sunset. It was like a dream. He was a so-called

evangelist according to our mother, Olla. This was the first time I ever

saw him, and, here he is, driving away. I thought to myself, I guess that's what preachers do. Marry someone, have kids. Then they get up

and go do the Lords' work. This is what I was being fed, only to discover

later a very, very different story altogether. Sadly, I did not find out

the whole truth about him until 2011. I'll talk more about that in later

chapters. I just want to point out, at this point in time, how strange it was

for Beth and I to see this come to pass without us really blinking an eye

and being more affected. When you are a child your values are different,

of course. Obviously, we, did not have much of an appreciation for family

in that era of our life. Why would we? Both of us were getting nothing

but strict, stern and abusive discipline. We couldn't help but see adults

as just another board, paddle, switch, confinement and chastisement

coming after us. Maybe deep down, I must have suspected our dad, to be

a threat. I never really did get to know what he was really like. I have only heard nothing but opinions, and, stories about him, through others.

It was becoming harder and harder to trust anyone as time un-

folded there in New Mexico. Uncle Robert and Aunt Kita were there for us

when mom was in need. We continued to attend his Church and school,

but, Robert had emphysema. It became alarming sometimes when

we would go over to see them,finding him in bed, extremely ill. The man

never did touch a cigarette his whole life. He passed away not too

long after we moved from Santiago. He was an exception. I trusted

that man to the bitter end. That couple loved our little family more than

any other acquaintances the entire time I was with Olla. They kinda took

center stage and filled a very empty void in our lives those days. That

couple was a very good example of truly loving Christians, who did not

need to use religion to cover up any kind of phony approach for monetary

gain.

It wasn't long before Olla thought it was necessary to break away

from Robert's so-called dominance. She decided to move to La Homa,

New Mexico for one more off the wall reason. She kept ranting and raving

about how Rob was always steering her in the wrong direction-that, it

was not Gods will. She could not have been more off beat. We surely

went through some unstable times when she flew the coop to get out

from under Mr. Crump's generous and loving wings.

It wasn't long after we arrived in La Homa that after falling

in love with a beautiful female neighbor, my age, across the street, Olla

decides to ship me off to a boys ranch again. I was twelve years old at that

point. Mom must have begun feeling more and more uneasy and insecure

trying to survive with two kids approaching their teen years. Again, it

seems like I was probably the one who ended up talking her into going through with taking me out of school to go to a place for boys that were

delinquents. At this time in my life, I did need a change to hold on to

my sanity with Olla, so unstable. Beth stayed with her this time, and, we

drove to South Fork, Oklahoma to meet Dr. Troy Jones. He was oddly

a some what of a jack of all trades. Starting out with a doctors License and

growing up on a farm, this man seemed to know how to pull quite a few

strings. He had been doing a lot of mailings to potential contributors in

hopes to fund his new project with donations. His idea started out

slow, but, it began to take shape shortly after we responded to his mail.

I wasn't clear, of course where exactly Mom got a hold of the information

about this ranch. I remember that we had a picture of the lakes on

the land he had purchased in South Fork, Oklahoma. Troy, was also an

ordained Minister and preached in the local church, there, close by. I was too young and ignorant to wonder or question what inspired him to be

so enthusiastic about founding a haven for wayward boys, that, had been

in trouble. Kids were convicted of assault, misdemeanor and some

felonies mostly in Oklahoma City, and Troy was in contact with the law

there. He hooked into the system somehow. He managed to take

on the custody role, welcoming the kids to his ranch and putting them to

work. Troy, had all kinds of projects going. He purchased a large piece of

land that had two lakes on it. It also included a few acres of crop soil,

plantable, and cultivated cotton fields. We planted & chopped cotton.

We all cut out potato buds and planted them by hand one day.

It turned out to be a successful crop of potato plants that year. We

never did have to irrigate. Troy, also seemed to be well versed in

psychology. He knew how to produce incentive for us fools. He always

seemed to come up with some kind of reward for all of our hard work which was exactly what kids need. He would inspire us with the idea of

chopping cotton for three weeks and promised to give us enough legal

tender to purchase a guitar and/or a 22' cal. rifle. Believe me, that, with

out a doubt, got our juices flowing like a river! I can't say enough about

the magnitude and power of that ingenious suggestion. We were

mesmarized. Whats more was, I, in true life, got my first guitar, there, at

age thirteen. There's no way I can explain with words what it meant

to work that hard for weeks in the humidity and heat, and, to be re-

warded with something that made such a sweet sound that connected us

all with the creative potential of the world. I was finally getting to the

point where I didn't feel so badly about leaving La Homa, and all the

bullies, in Santiago.

I was at the Lake Side Boys Ranch, twice. Only two boys were there in 1966 when I first arrived. Tom and Amos were a little older than I

was. They took me under their wing, were nice to me and they gave me a

good impression of the ranch life. It was surprising to find the two so well

behaved after being sent there by court order. I got a sweet taste of

the place. I was there a while, but, just as fate would have it, Olla,

I guess, found some reason to take me out. She was developing a love/

hate for the both of us siblings. I'm sure she felt guilty to a degree, and,

would end up taking advantage of the idea that she had custody of us.

I ended up coming back to New Mexico with her. She, then lived, in

Mohave after moving there from La Homa. I soon found myself having

to re-adjust at the schools and make new friends.

Mohave, New Mexico was a pretty cool little town. There is

a river that runs down the middle of that village, and I made some decent

friends there. For such a small place, it was a happening town because the economy was different in the sixties. There were multiple small farms

that produced a lot of alfalfa, hay and produce for the stores that pur-

chased a lot from the farmers. Then, there is 'Lake Flat Rock' a few miles

north that would draw a lot of tourists. Beth and I, now, well into our

teens, were surely headed for a venerable time in our young lives. I

seemed to continue to be a bully magnet. I am going to be sharing

a little more info, as this book progresses, about what exactly I was doing

and saying to kids. Things I fell victim to were, not at all, a mystery.

I was so stressed out from having to re-adjust so many times that I was

developing a jungle-spring-into-combat-mode reaction. I was beginning

to over-react to kids when they would tease me. By the time I hit

twelve years old I had already been in several schools, three children's

homes, two boys ranches and lived with a very unstable parent. The monster I felt inside was only being controlled by my ability to reach in to

my inner core and produce an imaginary friend. That second kid saved

my life over and over. He became superior. Nobody could live up to him

'cause he needed to be stronger and nicer than all those people that were

always trying to hurt me. I was becoming my own best friend, which was

good, but, I still wasn't winning peoples' respect. Kids were contin-

ueing to pick, on, *me*, especially. I always wondered, what on Gods green

earth was missing... I'll tell you what was missing: 'Humor!' I was never

around anyone who had a good, loose sense of humor. I saw clowns, and,

Red Skelton on Television. There was good humor all over and had been

for years, but, I wasn't seeing anything to be very laughable. I found a lot

of things pretty funny. The circumstantial oppression that I was being choked with, was unimaginable. The dark cloud was becoming some-

thing that I was too young to recognize, much less define it, or, see it.

I, of course got to liking Mohave, but unfortunately, I had be-

come so used to flying the coop, that, I guess I began to need to make a

major change to feel right. This stuff is crazy! I'm sure that, for some of

you, you would think that leaving town would be a welcome change.

For some families, a fresh start IS a good idea, but, it needs to involve a

business venture, now days, more than ever. Our mother was too bent

on following, or rather, seeking the so-called divine will of God. She

just wasn't taking advantage of any kind of free lance opportunities in the

business end of evangelistic enterprise. It was there in the sixties, and,

probably easier to initiate into motion back then, than it is now, with so

many people, out to sell God.

After re-adjusting to the elements and the new slew of kids in

Mohave, I began to go through some very memorable and important

changes. I was nine years old when we first moved there. We moved to

another children's home and we all moved back there when I was eight.

Olla, must have moved from apartment to house, to apartment, to house

three or four times. I especially got to liking the little green cottage that

is within walking distance from the Rio Grand River. I had met Kyle

Snow, who was my age at the elementary school there down the road. He

and I would go down to that river bank all the time and catch little Perch.

We would be so proud and happy to present the catch to our Moms. I

would actually enjoy cleaning the fish, and, we would feast. Both of

us would swim there too. We had some great times at that river.

The first time we lived in that town, I somehow, somewhere ran into a twenty one year old Hispanic friendly guy. He was funny. He was

generous. After some time he offered to take me for rides cruising the

boulevard, as there was so little going on in Mohave, NM. He knew

Kyle and the three of us would hang out together. 'Jesse Sanchez's

car was a 60s Ford Fairlane with a ridiculous over sized V8 engine. It

looked and sounded like shit, but, we had a blast pudding around town

with Jesse. He had a great sense of humor, and I loved hanging out with

older guys.

One night we dropped Kyle off at his house. I commenced

to ride with Jes after dark. To make a long story short, he was attracted to

young boys. He attempted to get into my pants several times. The

problem was, I just didn't have any kind or degree of sexual drive at age

nine. After he got to liking me a lot and showed sexual aggression, I found

it all to be pretty disgusting and I eventually let my mother know about his attempts. He was a cook at the local dinner down the road a piece.

Olla, was such a mooch. Jesse invited the 3 of us to his cafe one night for

dinner, on him. Mom was thrilled to eat out and not have to pay for the

meal. I didn't want to go. She couldn't figure out why I was being so nega-

tive about eating out. We got into the car, and I finally came out with the

news. When I told her Jesse was molesting me, she took the opportunity

to go ahead, eat the meal, *then*, she let him know to stay away. I, then, of

course, felt guilty and out of line. To top things off, he, later, verbally

attacks me in a chastising manner repeating over and over that I should

have told him to 'piss off,' and, "Why did you have to tell your Mother"?

Well, Dad, "Hello, I am a nine year old kid here." What did you

expect, for pity sakes"? I still liked the guy. He was very likable. What

kid wouldn't like soda pops, candy, laughs and rides all over town?

There I was, after living through serious abuse in three chil-

dren's homes, two boys ranches, almost died from Rheumatic Fever and

being raised, some of the time, by a very troubled and confused parent.

Now I'm made to feel like an idiot because I didn't know how to handle

another pedophile? I didn't mention the fifteen year old kid who basically

talked me, or rather coerced me into giving him oral sex in Texas. I

was so starved for hanging out with older children, male or female having

more to offer than being involved in sports or childish games. There were

many occasions, us kids, would resort to exploring our bodies' private

parts and peeping in windows trying to see someone naked in a shower.

Like most of us, the curiosity about sexual behavior can start when

kids are in elementary school, and/or before that, so, I wasn't exactly

wearing a little halo. I was curious about a lot of things. The birds and the bees was one of my many fascinations. I don't feel like I was

harmed in any way from the so-called sexual abuse and molestations that

I was involved with in my childhood. Nobody told me, that I should be.

We were moving around too much for me to remain focused on

any one subject to begin to be productive in something outside of, routine

living, if you will. It really takes a parent, or *someone,* to come up with an

idea, of quality, to hold the focus and profound interest of a child. This

was not the case for Beth and I. This is how people can get swayed and

waylaid. You can count on kids choosing to find their kicks that in-

volve theft or preying on a weaker victim. My suggestion to children

who are being pushed around and bullied or coerced into breaking the

law, is this: Communicate your worries to the right person. The one you

have found, before, that really listens. Communication break down, is, the single most haunting hang-up. It is THE reason people fall into, what I call

the 'pit puzzle.' If we are fed the wrong information at the starting gun,

the damage gets started before we have a snow-ball-chance-in-hell to

correct our aim. *Aim* and *focus* are so essential in any endeavor in order to

stay out of pit fall puzzles. Life is a puzzle, but it doesn't have to be a pit

fall. People are *not* born with a gift! Famous artists, singers & successful

business builders got to where they are, simply by, applying themselves.

If you are experiencing too many rocks in your road, and, if people

are standing in the way of your focus, let's try to figure out *why.*

Like I said, I wish we would have remained in Texas. Even worse,

Olla, pulled up roots, in Santiago, just when I began to adjust well there.

I loved the friends I had across the street. I was comfortable

in that big house on Center Avenue. The turmoil, I was yet to deal with, as my misguided childhood was unraveling, moving to the next

obstacle course, would become even more challenging. The gate, I was

headed for, and the bullies that seemed to gravitate into my direction,

proved to be getting a lot bigger, in comparison, to the bullies in

Santiago.

4

Meaner in oklahoma

If it was possible, I would erase most of the events that muddied

this part of my life. Lucky for you, I am going to share some very pertin

ent, special and sensitive information now-stuff that I spent a life time

learning the cowboy way. I found the hard way, was the best way, to be

honest. Believe me, my head is very full of pathetic stories. I promise I

will be short, so, I can continue to cut to the chase.

There are also some things about the martial arts that I want to

talk about in this collection also. I talked a little bit about Jesse in chapter

three. He was just one of the many individuals that I met and hung out with in Mohave. There was another guy there, that, Beth and

I would come to consider very influential, who did stand out above

the rest. His name was Axel Wade. We both got to feeling real good when

hanging around this guy, and, we learned from him. He was in his early

twenties. I can only begin to describe how much of a 'Joe Cool' Axel was.

He had the kind of personality that would draw you in. He had crazy hair,

and, was well built with a beer gut. Axel, was 'Mr. Personality.' Ironically,

in spite of the dumb-dumb that I was, he still took me under his wing

and, took an unselfish liking to the both of us. I felt that way, because,

most of the other teens and older guys we hung with, were all trying to

get into Beth's pants. She was a doll. Axel, was an exception. He was a

heavy beer drinker, but, he had this mysterious light around him. He re-

minded me of Dean Martin. He would take us fishing at the local lakes and good river fishing spots. He taught us how to use a bow and arrow, but,

maintained a comical approach with every scenario. Olla, even liked him!

He would stick up for me when bullies would come around, using more of

a diversion tactic, of a comical nature, than, being threatening to them.

Beth, and I just couldn't get enough of Axel Wade.

Wade was a part of a large family there in Mohave. I was in 6th

grade with his cousin Jordan. I was so disinterested in school there, that,

it's a good thing I did relate to some older kids, because, they were inevi-

tably who I respected and learned from. I was quickly learning, or, rather

choosing to be a self taught kind of guy. This was good, and... not so good.

Teachers would catch me day dreaming every day in class. I was seeing

people, places and things at face value at a younger age than most kids.

Needless to say, after what I had been through, and, going through at the time, you could expect me to be very different. Much of that started in my

toddler years. No one back then, read to me, and the adults, were always

doing everything but influencing me to take an interest in reading books.

I was becoming withdrawn and resorting to playing with toys. I was com-

pletly uninterested in school work, and, learning from anything written.

All the while, when I did live with Olla, I would ask her the meaning of a

word, or, how to to spell it. She would bark back, with telling me to find it

in the dictionary. She would spend hours in her room with a headache,

and/or reading the Christian Bible.

Children can be influenced quite easily. Parents can expect

children to decide what they want to do later in life between ages five to

eight. Olla, muddied the water when we were young. There was no need

to read, study, do well in school or prepare for the future, because according to her, Jesus was coming back to save us all, next month. I can't

emphasize enough how that idea, and way of thinking, sabotaged our

future as well as our day to day successes.

Children are so impressionable. Parents have tremendous impact

on kids. They are starved for food that works. If that food continues to

fit into the convenience of their life style, and feeds their physical, emo-

tional and psychological needs, they are going to hang on to that info.

People can be convinced easily, to believe something as way of life if an

adult got through to them on their level. I find this stuff really interes-

ting. The human mind can be manipulated so easily if someone does not

step in and take a stand. Cult leaders, have surely found ways to mass

hypnotize a bunch of suckers. It is because they've had so many seekers

and naïve followers, that, they stay in business.

I've found these Gurus' interesting, because, I too, was a victim

in every sense of the word. I was raised, being influenced, with an abso-

lutely ridiculous set of values. If you were never encouraged to dream,

you are not going to pursue a dream, because, you, were never taught the

the need to be creative. If your elders were not focused, then you started

out without a foundation, of which to build your structure.

I am going to begin to point out in this chapter, the need to work

on developing an aim, dream focus, and, why a lot of us are unfortunately

coming up short in that area. To start with, it is extremely important to

understand why religious cult leaders have such a stronghold on so many

eager spiritual believers. For one thing, people see it all, as real magic.

I spoke briefly about the void that we all feel, sometimes on a

daily basis. Others, just once in awhile. Homosapiens are lazy. We are living in a world of quick fixes, instant gratifications and tunnel vision.

This is world wide, not just in the U.S. are we succumbing these truths.

The only way we are going to control these behaviors is, to first know,

that they exist, and that, we are usually not even realizing that we are

inevitably being influenced.

One of the things I liked about Axel Wade was, that, he sure loved

being his own man. I don't think any guru could have ever been able to

talk Axel into participating in any kind of religious, or dominating way of

life.

Before I met Wade, I hung with a kid named Sam. His father

was the manager at the only Chevy house in Mohave. Sam's family

were doing better than most. They had trucks and motor bikes, and Sam,

would pick me up to go places pretty often. We had a great friendship

going.

I was at the Boyd's public swimming pool one day. One of Sam's

little brothers was giving me a hard time about something. I splashed

some water in his face. The next night he, and, his big brother came all

the way across town to push me around, drag me through the dirt and

humiliate me as if I beat somebody up or something. The older brother

became threatening in a very cruel manner. Sam just stood there and

watched. Needless to say the encounter pretty much ended the great

friendship I had with Sam. This would be just another common encounter

to add to my short lived relations with my young friends while I kept

needing, and, thirsting for something better. All the while I was becoming

less and less tolerant of rejection that only fueled my inability to be more

likeable so I could hold on to friendships and keep them. I was becoming meaner, more depressed and withdrawn. Beth, and I, both, were develo-

ping a temper to say the least. This was not the best addition to add to our

whacky lifestyle while we moved around so much.

I feel fortunate that I seemed to run in to people pretty often,

growing up, that were ahead of most people. Maybe I was simply more

open to the wisdom I learned from the many strangers that took an in-

terest in me. A lot of adults did see the rocky road I always seemed to be

on, and they wanted to help. Being offered tools and knowledge of how to

deal with the foe has been my greatest asset. I have always had more re-

gard for individuals that took a personal approach and, offered some

very concrete advice. For me that seemed to oil the squeaky wheel better

than what I learned in school, because I could apply the advice from face

value. I have always needed evidence and actual tools in order to hear, see and feel the resolve. The awesome power that lies within people. I began

to see it at a young age, and, in later chapters I have some information

about the power I was introduced to in Texas.

While growing up, I ran out of ideas about how to begin solving

bully dilemmas. I felt really alone. Beth, wasn't really affected like I was.

She had the empathy, but the poor girl was as confused as I was about the

issue. I just didn't know how to divert the subject and humor the situation

in a way to get along better with kids. I believe I could have had more

childhood friendships if I would have had better communication skills.

On the other hand some people want to fight regardless of what is on the

plate. There are no easy nor engraved in stone remedies for kids being

picked on. I have lived through it all, and, I do have quite a few sugges-

tions for the subject. Just hang on a minute while I break out my magic wand.

Seriously, there is always an answer to a need. There is usually a

way to deal with a negative. It is a matter of hanging in there long

enough to gather all the ingredients.

Beth, and I both began to hang out with Axel Wade & friends. His

drinking buddies were all fun. We loved those guys a lot. Beth, got to

where she was drinking us all under the table. She could drink an entire

beer all at once without a breather. We honestly had a good educational &

genuinely memorable time with Wade & friends. They were not a bad

gang, but, the alcohol abuse zipped up our fate pretty quick there in

Mohave. We came home way too many times half baked. Olla, damn

near went nuts. It didn't take her long to decide to pack it in and run

away from the subject at hand. Running away to solve a problem was really the only thing she knew to do. There we were, again, moving into

the infinite.

She found another apartment, but, she finally got a call from

Dr. Troy Jonathan. Before I could count to ten, mom, drove my butt back

up to Oklahoma, to return to his boys ranch. This was good. I did have

pleasant memories of the place. We arrived back there in 1967. I had just

turned thirteen, and, it was good to be back at first. Troy, had moved an

entire two story Victorian house in tact by tractor trailer on to the pro-

perty. He later had a replica of the 'Little Brown Church' of Iowa also

moved the same way right next to the closest lake there up from the

house. After returning to the place the second time, I was to discover

that Troy, had come up with a name for it,that, for a new boys work

ranch, it seemed to be the name that fit, and, stuck. After becoming official, 3 of us helped Troy with his address labels and envelopes to send

to potential contributors for the cause. Looking back, I have to give the

man a lot of credit for pulling that ranch together so efficiently and

effectively in such a short time. He networked with a lot of people there

in the area. Farmers and ranchers loved the guy. The primary reason that

he started the ranch turned out to be so shocking and out of character. I

was, eventually, to become absolutely spellbound to hear about Troy's'

habits. There were a whole lot of highlights, as well as dark events, that

took place during the two times I lived at Troy's boys ranch.

It was great to see new candidates there whom Troy had trans-

ported from Oklahoma City. He also found a family to help care for the

boys that fit in real well. Mrs. Luna, her son Ralph, and her daughter,

Sheila were hired to cook and maintain the place. The mom was patient with us. She loved the boys, and, she had a good heart. The family were

hard workers. Ralph, was nice to me, and he was responsible for surely

helping me to hold an interest in the guitar long enough to actually start

learning to play it when we all finally got a guitar.

After working in the fields chopping cotton for weeks to earn the

money for the guitars and the rifles, I must say, was certainly a motiva-

tion within itself. Ralph, was teaching us stuff like the riffs for 'Wipe Out',

'Day Tripper', 'Secret Agent Man', 'Louie Louie' and others. What was so

explosive, though, was that, we were also learning chords for songs we

could sing with that fit at the church where Troy co-pastored with

another guy. It only took a few weeks, and, we were already singing and

strumming the guitars for the people at the Sunday meetings.

Ironically, Troy would take 4 or 5 of us at a time rabbit hunting.

He used his 60s Dodge pick-up with spot lights on each side. Two of us would stand in the bed with our rifles resting on the cab. When we spot-

ted a rabbit it would sound like a war zone hearing the two semi 22 cal.

firing like a machine gun. Rabbits rarely got away. When we would see a

rabbit, it would always run in the direction we were driving. The rabbits

didn't have the sense to turn around south or haul ass back away from us.

Sadly we would end up with 10 to 15 jack and cotton tailed rabbits. Troy

would sometimes do his best to cook up a couple. He did not always have

the leasure time to make best of our kill. We eventually stopped hunting

so often for that reason, and it was surprising that Troy allowed us to

possess a firearm. These guys had been in trouble with the law, but, they,

of course were not exposed to the information about law like we are now.

The day came that this new haven I had been excepted and ad-

justed into, would take some disgusting turns. A very dark cloud floated over and rained on my parade the day Rizzio showed up. 'Rizzio, was

probably from some, south bronx shit hole, it seemed. Who knows, he

could have come from a well-to-do family.

Up to this point in my life, I thought I had seen and experienced

the meanest and worst bully. I was soon to find a whole new meaning of

the word. This guy, was the most unhappy, selfish, lazy, devious, con-

niving, dissatisfied, rude and ridiculous idiot, this world had ever pro-

duced. Rizzio was a piece of work. This poor guy didn't know the meaning

of love or friendship. He was incapable of adhering to practical or logical

advice. He was no doubt the sorriest individual I had ever met up to that

point. To top things off, I would, of course, be the one he would chose to

pick on, above the rest. He was meaner than I could believe.

I think by now you may see where I'm going with this. You will find one thing for sure if you keep reading. That is, that I am bringing out

all the attributes to the table about how and why I became the bully

magnet that I was. I can't emphasize enough how much better off I would

have been if I had only known just a few of the keys I am sharing with you

in this book.

What eventually made things go from bad to worse, was, the way

Rizzio would manipulate Troy, and, i find out years later, that there was

an underground reason they got along, so well, to boot.

To our surprise, Troy walked in one day, and said: OK boys, a

man is coming out today to dig a hole to bury a cellar. He networked with

a couple of guys to install a full sized freight train rail road box car

completely underground. He said we need it for a fall out shelter, and, to

store food. The guy he knew somehow managed to get it on to a tractor

trailer and haul it all the way from, who knows where. It all fell into place and, was a success. Before we knew it, we were down there inside getting

picked on by Rizzio. We never did have to escape any tornadoes though.

The ranch life continued to be fun and rewarding. Things were

going smoothly up until the day we were all sitting around listening to

Paul Harveys' news broadcast, Troy's' favorite commentator. I walked in

to the kitchen to talk to Sheila. I then came back out to the living room.

Rizzio comes up from behind in a fit of rage, and strikes me in the middle

of my back. It was a direct hit on the mid-spinal area. This was not just a

punch to get my attention. This was a full blown blunt force closed fist

attack from behind. It knocked the wind out of me. I got up and ran

toward the lake. I fell to my knees and eventually composed myself. When

I was able to breath, Rizzio, walks out and did nothing more than threaten

me, not to blow the whistle.

I had been in such dire straits to be excepted by this guy, and the

other boys, that, I agreed to keep the incident in the closet. This was a

typical example of the insecurities I suffered. I got an x-ray after having

back pain years later, and, found that I developed a spur on my spine

in the place where I was hit that day. Beth, and I have dared to be any-

thing but the hypochondriac our mother seemed to be. She would go to a

chiropractor or a doctor with the slightest ailment. She did not work out,

jog, nor, attend any physical therapy training or classes. Olla, was al-

ways claiming to be sick, and, when I would take a job or have a tough

time at school, while living her, she would advise me. She would always

say: "Well just tell 'em you're sick!

Our poor mother had a whole slough of problems. It's really, no

wonder why she kept placing us in the boys ranches & children's homes.

I must tell you how proud I am to admit, that, I have surely insisted on

being my own doctor, practicing and believing in self healing. I am here

today with back pain, but, a long ways from being out of commission.

I could go on about Rizzio, and all of the scenarios of those days

when he kept picking on me, but, I have plenty more information to share

about more productive subjects.

Strangely enough, Troy, had won the love and respect of a lot of

members of his church. Anyone that has attended any kind of organized,

religious group can agree that it is common to establish camaraderie

and trust. People trusted Troy, because he was involved with a rock solid

cause.

To top things off, Troy, would ask us to pack a bag and get ready

for an out of town visit. He had a 1967 Plymouth VIP, and, he would pile in 3 and 4 of us kids for an out of town trip to visit a few of his church

members at their homes and farms. Sometimes he would show up una-

nnounced, and these people would always welcome him with open arms

anyway. They would feed us and put us up for the night.

    We visited a family one afternoon that cooked an elaborate meal

for us. We all sat in the living room on their sheet-white sectional. Things

were going great until I knocked over my glass of pure purple grape juice,

not just on to the couch, but, on to the white carpet, to boot. The wife

rushes in with a bucket of soap/water. The poor woman gets down on her

knees and scrubs, and, scrubs, and, scrubs. She continues to work tire-

lessly to, no avail. The soap didn't even dilute the grape juice.

    As young and ignorant as I was, I still felt really bad for this

woman. I was clueless. There was nothing I could do, to, undo the

accident. They must have forgiven us. It was bad enough, but, of course,

Rizzio would make me go from, feeling like a klutz, to make me want to

walk the plank for the rest of the trip.

We continued to visit more farmers and members of the church.

Troy, was allowing all of us to take turns driving the car. I felt privileged

to have access to so many different vehicles. After driving the tractors,

the motor bike, the motor boat and now Troy's Plymouth, I felt like a

team player with people waiting for me to perform. I got so much driving

experience from such a young age, that, I have managed to capitalize on

driving safety, enough to share, my knowledge with others.

The one trip we took not long before I left the ranch, was the most

significant. We went to visit an older guy somewhere in north Texas who

lived way out of town by himself. He lived in a single story stucco

Mexican style ranch house that was surrounded with fences. There was

not a perimeter walkway. It was impossible to jog or walk around his house without having to open up and go through a bunch of fences.

That night he shared a great meal with Troy, the boys and me. The man

told us a little bit about the activities going on there while he was there

alone at night. He said he had been awakened several times by the sound

of someone picking up his kitchen silverware and slamming it against the

walls. He also heard closet and cabinet doors being opened and shut

real hard several times. The story he came up with after that, we all sure

thought, had to be a bunch of non-sense. I had forgot about the stiflingly

horrific experience I had in Washington when I was two. If you were to

ask me, those days, if I believed in ghosts, I would have had to say no. The

man continued to share with us the details about the noises he kept

hearing mostly at night there on his ranch. He continued with another, hard to believe, scenario. The man went on to try to explain, to the five of

us, what else he kept hearing at night. We all really thought the guy was

just coming up with a bunch of stories to humor the evening arousing

our curiosity. He said he would hear several horses galloping around the

house loud enough to wake him out of a deep sleep. According to him this

had been going on for several months.

   We all finally went to bed that night with difficulty getting to

sleep. I kept looking out the window hoping to see the invisible horses.

We all laughed and joked about the poor ranchers' phenomenal sightings.

Later, after we all were real close to falling asleep, the curtain in the

window began to move back and forth. I thought right away, this can't be

right, because, I was sure there was no wind, nor even a slight breeze that

night. Suddenly the window made a noise, and, the curtain started swaying back and forth erratically. Three of us were half scared out of our

underwear to the point of jumping on Troy, in his bed to wake him

up. We turned on the light only to find that Troy, had tied a string to the

curtain, and, had been pulling the string back and forth the whole time.

I was relieved, but angry at Troy, of course. After hearing all that the

rancher had shared with us, this, was just too much for us stupid teen-

agers. I felt so dumb, but, what the heck. At least it was not a real ghost,

and, that was just fine with me. We never heard the horses, nor did we

hear the kitchen noise. We went on down the road never really thinking

much more about the whole ordeal. Those days, I think, most people

thought of that sort of thing to be made up, and, a fallacy.

The five of us drove back to South fork and spent the night at

Troy's home there. Rizzio, continued to squawk about his ordeal with getting along with Troy. He, was telling us things that were just too

hard to believe, so, we all kept writing him off and ignoring him. This did

not serve him well, and, he just got meaner. He would rarely tell the truth

so, we discontinued to believe, most everything that he said.

After a couple more trips out of town, we noticed an unusual

looking car parked in the dirt lot there next to the Victorian house, at the

ranch. The hired hand walked up to the car and whispered something in

Troy's ear. We all got out of the car to find a real tall skinny stranger

standing there with a guy from Mexico. The two men were opening the

trunk of the car revealing a large load of watermelons. I turned to look

a little closer at the tall guy, and, realized it was my dear ole dad. I

didn't even recognize him from a worn out picture that my mother had.

I seemed to know it was Ansel. I only saw him once before, but, he looked

different that time. It had only been four years.

I don't even remember talking to my father at the ranch this

time. I just remember him explaining how to hold your fist when you are

going up against an opponent in a boxing match. I also recall him prea-

ching a sermon there at Troy's church, and, having me to stand up. He

came up with the idea that he was having trouble supporting his family.

He wanted to make sure that members of the church witnessed that I did

in fact, exist. According to his strategy and purpose, he claimed to be

supporting us, and, he needed help and contributions. I didn't think much

about what was really going down, at the time, as young as I was. The

irony of the whole subject with Ansel was,that, he turns out to be the

shock jock of the century. What he was really doing between Mexico and

the United States was absolutely the last thing I would have ever guessed.

I can't wait to reveal all the ironic information about what Ansel was up to in later chapters, so, you will understand why he wanted so little to do

with us. Beth, got on the computer back in 2010 and found some interes-

ting information about Ansel's military profile status. Records showed us

for the first time that he had been injured in the army. He got a medical

discharge after his legs were severely burned in a training accident while

stationed in some crazy installation back east. We both think that Olla

may have known about it, but, did not reveal what she knew to us. It al-

ways appeared to us that she was really bent on making him look like the

bad guy of our broken family. It sounds like to me she needed to make

him look bad so she would look good. Not a good influence, raising kids.

Ansel, stuck around for a day or two, but, soon rode off again into

the sunset, headed to, who knows where. It was truly a memorable experience to see him a second time. I wondered why he was exceptionally

bilingual in the favor of Espanol. I was curious too about why he kept

returning to Minnesota after preaching the so-called gospel in Mexico.

I am pretty sure that Ansel, heard us when we played songs in the

church. I must say, that, if it wasn't for my new found love for the things

we found to do with our guitars, I think I would have gone off the deep

end. With Troy, being such a prude, and, Rizzio such an idiot... music

is surely what saved my neck. I will be the first to tell you, that, a musical

instrument can be a form of meditation. You don't have to be a successful

superstar to get the most out of the instrument. It can be your best friend.

Sometimes a secret friend like a guitar can be the escape we need to turn

the world off for a few minutes in our time of needing to get control of our sanity. I can't say enough, about how important it is, to network

with others if you want to do something serious with publishing your

songs.

I guess I must have remained at the boys ranch for another year

after Ansel paid his visit. We continued to plant potatoes, hunt cotton

tail & jack rabbits, chop cotton and tolerate Rizzio for as long as I can re-

member. Mrs. Luna, her daughter Sheila and son Ralph stuck around

for a surprising length of time. We all had so much fun in the two lakes

there on the property. They were full of water moccasins and snapping

turtles, but, none of us ever got bit nor attacked while swimming. Most

reptiles are more likely to run the other direction. We felt so damn lucky.

That lake was the one thing we sure did look forward to after working all

day in the fields. I did a lot of growing up at the boy's ranch. I was there every bit of thirteen months, but, I surely do have some fond

memories of the place. I inevitably connected with nature, there, in it's

purest form. I was unaware of all that back then, but, I know I was surely

learning to be my own best friend, and, finding grace in music. I received

a lot of gratification from the simplicity of the summer days there in

beautiful Oklahoma.

Troy, had hired a teacher to conduct a home-school approach to

our educational needs. He must have been trying to keep us out of the

public schools for his isolated reasons. Troy, was an odd-ball, and, it does

not surprise me that he tried to keep us in a private class room. This may

be a part of the reason Olla, came back to take me out of the boys ranch.

She had moved again, on to an Indian pueblo in west New Mexico. I do re-

member being glad to see her, and, willing to journey back with her again simply because, I was so tired of being dominated and picked on by Rizzio.

I figured I had dealt with the worst bullies, before I had reached this boys

ranch. I've got to tell you, though, I surely found Rizzio and others, to be

a lot meaner, in Oklahoma.

5

APACHE / BLUE ROCK

Again, Olla, moved to another town, while I was in South Fork,

Oklahoma. When I heard she moved on to an Indian reservation, being

the curious and open minded kid, I had become, I found it exciting. She

dropped in for a visit at the 'Lake side Boys Ranch' where I was at the

time. After hearing her talk about the Apache Indian town, I guess I must

have ended up talking Olla into taking me with her to live there. She

rented a trailer, and, I tried to blend into the school where she de-

cited to teach. It was a religious institution called 'Oxahaca Mission.'

I was supposed to be in 8th grade, but, they started me off in 7th because

the home school, I was in at the boys ranch, did not measure up to the

missions' requirements. There again, I was set back a grade, and, that did

not do my ego and self esteem a lot of good.

The students were mostly, Caucasian. There were a few Navaho

kids also. As hard as it was to believe, there were no mean kids in the en-

tire class I was in. The place only went up to 8th grade, and the same

teacher taught the 6,7th and 8th graders in the same class room. The

teacher was a guy from back east. He had lived and taught school in

London, England prior to his job there at Oaxaca. I'll never forget

him showing us a film of his son, talking, after being there for six months.

He was born in the U.S. but, had developed a complete English accent

in the short time they had lived in London. Then, he quickly lost the

accent after moving back to the U.S.

I took a liking to the kids there in that school right away. I found

it to be extremely odd to, *not*, run into any bullies. I found it to be a

lot easier to be nice to people when they were nice to me. Like

I mentioned in earlier chapters, I had already begun to develop a mean

streak & a temper that was the result of way too much negativity in every

sense of the word. The influence I had been subjected to would take

50 years to get a handle on. I only wish I could change the way I

did treat people. Sadly, it takes a combination of insight and checking

your look in the mirror. I want to point out, to you now, something

that I had to learn only by living it, and that is, that, *you got to love your-*

self. We have to like ourselves, and approve of our self before we can like

others. I know, that sounds like a cliche' you may have heard before. I

I want you to know, I spent a life time of NOT liking, nor excepting myself.

My self esteem was in deep trouble, and, I was forever having to learn

these things, the cowboy way.

There was one kid there at Oxahaca, that took a liking to me in-

spite of all of my short comings. He was full blooded Navaho, and, he was

from a large family that lived in Blue Rock. This little village was sort

of an extension of Apache. It was about 5 miles East. This little guy, who

brought out the best in me, invited me over to his family house numerous

times. The father bought the kids a Honda 305. Surprisingly, that family

allowed me to ride the stupid thing all over Blue Rock. I had the time of

my life on that bike, and, the parents did not nag about anyone speeding

or abusing the privilege. I felt so free and uninhibited. I got to loving that

family so much. They all made up for my bicycle getting stolen earlier.

It got swiped soon as I landed in Apache. I did finally find my bike. It had been stripped and used for parts. I got the frame back, and, talked Olla

into purchasing tires and parts for it. She was impressed that I managed

to restore the bike with minimal tools and parts, but, nothing compared

to the Honda in Blue Rock. I kept getting rides there from Apache. I hung

out with some older teenagers that had a an old Volks Wagon bug. It was

the ride to Blue Rock from Zuni when I first heard 'Lady Madonna' by the

Beatles. I'll tell ya, those were some happy and cherished days.

It finally snowed while my short stay in Apache. The family

invited me to come, discover and share the fun they all had each year

sledding down a mountain road just north of the village. We would get to

going really fast down that steep road. I just loved that little Navaho kid.

I can't even remember his name, but we had a lot fun, on that hill.

Olla decided to move again shortly after winter. She found

a ground level apartment on the out skirts of town. It was a nice place, and, we met one of the teachers there that had a good looking daughter

with whom I, right away, felt inferior. I, somehow knew I would never live

up to her expectations, and, with that kind of leg to stand on, I totally did

really blow one night. We were invited to an arts & crafts workshop.

It was the first time I came close to actually going out with this girl. We

were chosen to work together on a project making something out of the

material the club was furnishing. I was the one chosen to be the first

to stand up and explain what, and how we constructed our project. Well...

I had always had stage fright, of course. I was completely new to talking

to an audience. In fact, I had *never* got up to speak to a crowd this big,

and, oh my God! I stood up and, Yikes, I could not think of anything to say

to tell the people what we were doing. I never dreamed anybody would pick me first. So, I stood there and pointed at the picture, we made saying

nothing! The place went silent. You could have heard a pin drop! Mean-

while, the girl I had partnered with, was falling apart. This really em-

barrassed her, way worse, than what I was going through. I did manage to

mumble a few broken words. A question was asked, and I remember be-

ginning to relax, but, it was too late. That girl would never talk to me with

any kind of respect after that night, just to really twist the killing knife.

Hell, I already felt like less of a human being around her, but, that night

sure did seal my chances of ever winning her selfish love. Ha... I don't

think I missed much.

Sadly, it was at that apartment complex where I fell back in to

becoming withdrawn again and reaching into my one single ability to

cope. That was; to refer to the guy within, that excepted me unconditionally, and was my own best friend.

I used to wonder what my buds at the Boys Ranch got out of

smoking cigarettes. I was beginning to drift into a direction away from

purpose. I was thirteen just reaching puberty. Our mother, was just not on

my side, nor teaching me much about how to handle depression. She had

always come at me with the Jesus thing in a very aggressive and forceful

way. It was doing nothing for me, except to drive me away and in to

trying to fill the void. The void that was growing larger and harder to

understand. For the first time, I tried smoking cigarettes. It first made

me extremely dizzy. Like most of us, it relaxed me, and seemed to

help me to control the, monster void I had always felt especially around

our mother. Both Beth and I, back in New Mexico, were always feeling

empty and broken inside as a child. We were so trapped. I ended up smoking on a daily basis there for while. I would either smoke with a

friend from school. or I would ride my bike to a remote sandy hill area &

smoke alone. Surprisingly, I did not continue to smoke habitually. It was

just too hard to get by Olla who would always beat me with a board if she

smelled tobacco in my cloths. She kept hitting me in the face.

Beth, at this time, while I was living with mom in Apache, had al-

ready been enrolled in the boarding institution called Durango school.

I was just hearing about 'Durango' for the first time in 1968. It sounded

like my sister had adjusted and settled in well there in Hermosa, NM.

Durango, had a good reputation. Or, at least this is the message the

authorities attempted to convey to prospective students. In a lot of ways,

the school had a unique reputation for success in excepting kids and

processing them through the four years. If you graduated from there, you had to show some courage, drive and determination. The thing that I

found out about Durango, years later, was something I should have been

told before enrolling. Beth, told me some stuff that was horrifying for me

to believe. It did it make a lot of sense, and clarified the events that went

on there that I need to discuss after you and I figure out why I was so

lost after graduating from there.

Like so many villages and the towns Olla tried, Apache, did not

prove to be the land of milk and honey. It wasn't long before she

decided to move on. This time, it was back to Mohave. We had been

there earlier long enough to establish some friendships and planted our

feet, so to speak. She got back to her churchy good friends, that never

really excepted her, and we continued to attend the little church on the

hill just off of U.S. Highway 95. We had lived in a small cabin that was built to look like it was made of logs. It was one of the places Olla rented

when we lived in Mohave, NM. This time Olla, found a place across

town, and, Beth came home for the summer vacation. We got back to-

gether with Axel Wade, and friends, again, shortly after we all got settled

in the place mom rented. Beth, wrote me from Durango with some

enthusiasm. I began to relish the idea of enrolling there myself. Mean-

while, the both of us were becoming a couple of misguided, misdirected,

impatient, rebellious and curious teenagers. We snuck out several

times and partied with the older kids who were old enough to

purchase beer. We had to drive 12 miles out of town to get it, being

a dry county. Ironically, we all ended up back in the cabin we used to live

in with Olla. Axel, and another guy happened to see it for rent. So, there

we were later on in life, partying in our old childhood rental, and, man did we hoop it up. Good night Irene, Ooo wee, Yee,haw, & Ride em cow-

boy! We would get so drunk. Beth, could drink all of us under the table.

She could knock off a whole beer, all with one breath. I could never match

that. We continued to enjoy the gang we hung with a little too much. Here

we were, Beth fifteen, and, me thirteen-drinking alcohol with no

direction home. We would return at night to Olla, and, she only made

things worse. Which was the whole reason we were needing to get our

kicks outside of the home. She just wasn't an artsy- craftsy type person,

nor were either of us, very inspired. She was depressed. The religion

was just not fixing her engine, as much as she wanted to believe, that

it was. The fanaticism was doing nothing but separating us from any

kind of communication with her. She kept quoting scripture and calling

both of us 'the Devil'. This behavior was only escalating. We were still just kids. The only thing I could think of, as a way out, was to try to get her

to agree to place me in another boys ranch or children's home.

Things were heating up after 1968. Beth, had spent the summer with us

in Mohave, after her first year at Durango. We were due for a change,

and, it needed to be a positive one.

Olla, kept insisting we attend meetings at the little rock church

on the hill next to U.S. Highway 95. I got to where I would've rather been

thrown into a pit of rattle snakes. To my amazement, this is when I had

found the privilege of meeting someone there that would forever alter my

life.

Joe Duke, Joe Duke Wilson, was a very intense kid. He had a speech

impairment, and, he seemed a little eccentric, if you looked at his darker

side. I had no way of identifying what was really going on with this

precious kid. We seemed to hit it off. He was from the next little town,

North West, off Hwy 95. It wasn't long after I met Joe Duke, that Olla, got

a little closer to a couple of the women there at the church. They began

inviting us to their homes for prayer meetings 43 miles north of that area.

Our relations with these folks progressed, and, we began to visit several

Christians there. We would see them often. As time rolled on, and I soon

turned fifteen, I got the chance to drive around the little city with Joe D.

He lived with his aunt Samson, there. His father was a truck driver and

drank a lot. Joe Duke, was, sort of, in the same class I was. The Samsons

were well off ranchers, but, the poor kid was just not very content with

the arrangement. He loved his Dad, but, his father 'Luis Wilson' was

not very dedicated, and, I was to find out later just how much Joe Duke

was affected. The depression he was suffering was not apparent.

I wouldn't have known how to identify it, as a kid, back then any way.

We were, blowing it, in Mohave. Mom did not approve of the

gang we were hooked up with, and, both of us were, little by little, be-

coming dependent on the booze. I got to where I didn't even care for

that little hick town. I had finally made some good friends there, but, we

couldn't really hang with them. Olla, decided to up-root again. I found

myself again,wishing we had never left, Apache / Blue Rock.

6

THE LOS LUNA HOOK

Discovering the next small city, while still in New Mexico, Beth

and I, were happily surprised, to find a place, that was uniquely different.

These were the days that it was extremely unusual to find, in the late 60s

and 70s, a happening, hot, busy, friendly, hip little party town. I got a very

good impression of the place. The first thing I became hooked on was

doing nothing but driving & riding in a zigzag, from one end of town and

back. Joe Duke, borrowed his uncle Hank's 1966 Ford long bed pick-up

just about every day. The truck was red and white. It stuck out like a

LOU ENZO MAYSON

sore thumb, but, he and I had the time of our teenage lives driving that

stupid looking Ford all over every street in town, lookin' for kicks. His

cousin, Irene, had a gorgeous friend named Abbie. She was a little older

than me by a couple of years, but, it wasn't long before she would surely

have nothing to do with me. I found out early on, that I, not only had little

to offer a girl, but, I had no class. I just didn't know how to get a gal

to like me. This was not good,'cause this girl was a doll. I wanted this

woman so bad. With my ridiculous manners, she dumped me. We all

gotta start somewhere. It only took me a life time to learn how to keep

from repelling women.

    John Ranger, was probably the biggest bully I had ever dealt with

my whole life. He also had a crush on Abbie. When he found me on a date

with her, at a ball game at the high school there, during basket ball season he went nuts. We were on our way back to the car, when, at the last

minute, he runs up and grabs me, picks me up and throws me into the

dirt parking lot like a rag doll. He must have weighed 250. I was every bit

of 140 lbs. He picks me up, throws me against a car and says: "The only

way I can ever fix this is to"... as he produces a full powered right hook

into my pathetic face. The guys I was with, managed to pull him off. He

finally collects himself. We got back in the car without too much dam-

age. The company, Abbie, and I, were with, drove around town for a while

preceding our encounter with Ranger. Before long, we had a car follow

us for quite a while. We stopped, and out- jumps a gang of Los Luna team

members. One guy comes up to the window and says: "Hey gringo, we had

to control Ranger. He gave us a hard time, and because of you, we had to fight him." Now, think about this. Here I am with a girl everybody wants,

and, these guys are saying that I should have fought my own fight. I was

spellbound. I thought, what was I missing? Wow, does that make any

kind of sense? From that night on, three of those guys had it in for me,

and continued to harass and threaten me, at every encounter. My

question again, why am I an instant bully magnet? For once, I was actually

making friends and enjoying the new town. I think I, was getting a

taste of what the women and children have to deal with in the middle

eastern countries. It all started off very bitter, sweet.

The Duke, and I, hung out together a lot. He was a breath of fresh

air. I did not have a car, and, I depended on him too much. This added to

his discontentment and depression. I didn't see any other way, at the

time, to escape the wrath Olla, kept incumbering both Beth & I with, but, that was nothing new. We both, were becoming less and less tolerant.

Like always, when things started getting rough, mom would move

again. She found another rental across town. I was tired of moving every

three to six months, but, this time would prove to be the last move we

made, living with Olla. We discovered a restaurant close by on route 66

with in walking distance. I chose to take on my first job there as a cook

side help. I hated having to be there at 5am every day, but, I met Dolly

there. Dolly Martinez, was so nice to me. She became a mentor. She would

even allow me to borrow her 1967 Ford Fairlane. Dolly happened to be

the girlfriend of Joe Duke's, Dad. I would return home each day finding it

more and more difficult to get along with Olla. I would jump, angerly

back in to that poor car and speed off like the devil. It's a wonder I did not get pulled over. I did have a class C drivers license, but, I was just too

stressed and angry to drive someone else's car.

Beth and I had, had enough. Our mom had turned into the worst

nagger this side of Texas. I was still, just fifteen. Beth, now seventeen,

applied to rent an apartment about two miles away and qualified. It

was small one bed room. At first, we both moved in there together, but,

come the end of summer, Beth was off, back to Durango. I was

left to make the doughnuts and pay the rent. However, to top things off,

when I attempted to enroll to the high school down the street, the

principle there denied me enrollment. He thought it to be unacceptable

for a teenager to live away from his parents, work, pay rent and function.

I got so angry. I loved the school for some reason. I just wanted to be

normal, and a regular Joe. This rejection was not good. This meant going

back to live with Olla, or, go enroll at Durango, 95 miles away. I chose to attend Durango School. The Principal there, I think, liked Olla,

and, I felt like Forest Gump that day, but, I was excepted. Joe Duke, was

also there, and, I managed to blend in, so to speak, but, I was, to quickly to

find out, that, I may as well have been dropped off in Vietnam.

I will never forget the day Beth and I were taken on a tour

the first week of school there in Hermosa, New Mexico. It was my fresh-

man year. Beth was a junior. The guys all loved her, but, it was not the

same for me, of course. Durango was, and, still is a boarding school. There

were things back then, I did not know about. What I was about to learn,

were things, that really had a negative impact on the lifestyle that I would

choose after graduating. My time at Durango was a lot like the events

that took place in the movie 'Bad Boys' with Sawn Penn. I just couldn't

prepare myself enough for the hate and violence that plagued my status trying to fit in with some of the students in the dorm. The dorm super-

visor there, was, for one thing, not very empathetic. He was out to bust

and severely punish you, if you proved to be delinquent and out of hand

or a trouble maker. Houser 'Mr. Houser' was a piece of work. He was

Caucasian, and, he had mean streak. He was a whimp, in comparison

to several of the Hispanic students whom were street fighters from the

get-go. Bullies always know who they can target by how you handle your-

self. They delight on continuing to pick on you when they identify

what pushes your buttons. If you prove to react with a defensive spring-

back-jungle-mode, they are gonna love you, because you are giving them

the ammunition and the excuse to hurt you, as much, as they possibly can

get away with. I, at the time, had no idea that I was simply loading

their guns. These guys picked on me on a daily basis for months. One day one guy would accuse me of flirting with his girlfriend. The next day,

another would call me a fagot, I would react negatively, and I would soon

be on his shit list. I just did not know how to humor the situation. All I

needed to do was, turn the idea around, and joke with these guys daily.

They are just bored and looking for kicks. They are, obviously suffering

a social anxiety disorder. It's up to you to bring out the better person

that IS, in place. It just needs to be stimulated with a positive and exciting

approach that they can actually benefit from. Children are not born with

a set of good values. If kids are not given reasons to see their parents as

God, and, if they do not love and admire you, they are going to find solace

acceptance with their peers. That, unfortunately, can involve kids that

form a gang that can surely turn strange. I was lucky. I was forced into becoming my own gang member. We moved from town to town so often

that I just shied away from gangs and clickish groups. The solace I had

discovered within myself was the only thing I had to cling to. To

some degree, it was a good thing. At the time, it was the only thing, Beth

and I really possessed.

I need to continue to cut to the chase on this subject. The terror

I was affected by, came to boiling point, and I want to make this story

as short as I possibly can. I don't want my readers to miss the point that

I am trying to make about bullies. All I needed to do is look at one

of these guys' girlfriend, and, I soon had a monkey on my back. One after-

noon, one of these guy's, told me he was going to meet me in my room,

for a confrontation. Well, come 7pm there must have been fifteen good

buddies come into my room to watch the little gringo get beat up.

Joe Duke, and I, had made a tent out of blankets that surrounded our playful bunk beds. I was in bed inside the tent when they all came

in uninvited. 'Jose, the top dog(I forgot his last name) hollered come out

and fight like a man. All of these a-holes knew quite well I was not into

going up against any of them in a dual. What is totally ironic about

this situation is that, Jose, was trained for years in Karate. He was not

just a street fighter. He knew Martial Arts. He reaches in and yanks me

from the bed to the floor. While my head rested face up against the

hardwood, he comes down with a full force right hook into my right eye.

Blood gushed out of my face. There was so much blood that I used it as

lubricant to slide under the bed across the room while he continued to

rib kick me to try to show me who was boss, I guess. When the audience

realized the depth of the attack, I was told later, they all bailed out of

the room like a bunch of scared rabbits. When the smoke finally cleared, I composed myself enough to get to the latrine. As I was cleaning up, Jose,

comes in and says: "You know, there comes a time when a man has to ad-

mitt his mistakes, and this time I was wrong." He never apologized, but,

he came to a swift conclusion that he had made a serious error.

The strangest aspect about the ordeal with my good buddies, at

Durango, in 1970 is, that, the principle was evidently so intent on reaping

benefits. That guy must have been so concerned about maintaining the

census, that he over looked the attack. He seemed to look at me as the

instigator. Three of the group were real apologetic there in the office that

day. One of them said something, to the tune, that I offended them.

I think what he really meant was, that, my being there as a nice looking

peaceful Gringo, offended them.

Mister Knight, Principle, dismissed us all that afternoon. My eye was black and swollen shut. I staggered out of there wondering if I was in

war zone or somethin.' It sure seemed like a civil war. I was just a pathetic

casualty, starting off, a conscientious objector. Laws have tighten up

since those days, but, people still get away with this stuff now.

Bullies are much more likely to retaliate with a gun before they even

graduate high school. When the day finally came for me to move

on after finishing those four years of hell, I was worst off than before I

began.

I was aimless when I graduated. I was a lot more lost than

most people. Beth had got out, away from Durango a couple of years be-

fore I did. She and Derek, drove up to Durango, that day, to take me back

to our so-called home. It was great to be out of school. I never did blend

in. If I read anything up to that era of my life, it was only because it was

absolutely necessary. I just did not see the need to read. Not good.

Beth, married Derek around the time she graduated from

Durango. I had met Derek 'Derek Nava Gallegos,' and became close

friends with him before he met Beth. We had already become drinking

buddies, and, we had a few things in common. The two had rented a

trailer and parked it next to his parents. You can imagine how that went.

I had met several unforgettable, sweet people, there in Los Luna, long

before I had graduated at Durango. There were so many that, several of

them, became the most cherished acquaintances of my entire life. To

this day, I continue to attempt to stay in touch with them.

Not too long after I fell in lust, with Abbie, I, fortunately met Jake.

Jake Hanson. This is one guy who really stands out above the rest.

He always seemed to be ahead of all of us with room to spare, and, was all-

ways the 'Joe Cool' of the friends I had. Jake & I did go to school together, but, my fondest memory of him was the times we hung out at his mom's

place. She drank beer while we smoked pot and listened to Grand Funk

Railroad. This was a very unique ritual, something I never really came

that close to enjoying with Olla. Jake's Mother 'Annie' was just, com-

pletly cool. She was not a disciplinarian. She was far from religious. She

had been a hard worker, and you could tell she really loved her three

kids. They all respected her. All three kids grew up to be very loving

and exceptionally bright. Jake had a light around him that really drew

you in. We had so much fun together, and, we shared much in common.

I did feel inferior around Jake. He seemed to be decades ahead of me.

Jake seemed to be in tune with all of the newest musical pop artists. He

introduced me to the first Cheech & Chong album. I admired and envied

his whole family very much. I just could not get enough of this guy.

Jake was his own man. He did not hang with the local gangs,

clicks, groups or crowds. I guess you could say that's why I related to him.

We both were in the army for the same amount of time, and we got out

after three years, in September, 1975. It was a great year, and, we didn't

plan those dates. The two of us really did share some special things in

common. We both had a sister the same age. They both got married and

raised a boy and a girl that hung out together. Jake, and I were both

regular army. We were both in at the same time for three years. Both of

us grew up without a father, and neither of us were inclined to get a

college degree. Anybody starting their life out in small towns back in the

70's were subjected to a pretty unambitious approach. Even if parents

tried pushing kids to become somebody or to study and get a vocational

trade, it didn't work so well, if they, were not setting an example. I tell people now, the world I grew up in, no longer exists.

Joe Duke, also, returned to Los Luna, after we all got out of

high school. I think it was that summer that his dad invited him to

journey up to Colorado. I just got off the phone with Jake tonight. I've had

Joe Duke, in my thoughts, these past few days. When conversing with Jake

this time, I asked if he remembered him. He said that he was never very

fond of Joe Duke after having a horrible dream about him. Jake, for the

first time, told me about his nightmare of riding in a car with several

other people. Joe Duke, was driving, and, he drove the car off the road

on purpose possibly with the intention of taking every one in the car with

him. After my chat with Jake, I thought, WOW! In the early 70s, Joe Duke,

continued to ask me, **not** to come with him because he had another friend

in Colorado that he related to. He said, he also did not think, I would fit

in. I was disappointed. I was offended, and, I wanted to go.

About three weeks later I get a call from Beth, when she worked

at the news office there, in Los Luna. She explained that she had some

bad news about Joe Duke. She said it would be better if she was absolutely

certain about his status. All she had heard up to that point was, that a car

was spotted plunging off the road and exploding into pieces in rocks a-

bove the trail near a high peak, miles from Denver. Duke, at that point,

had been missing, but, I knew he was gone. I knew it, because he had

talked about suicide several times to me. He had even said that, the kid he

knew in Colorado was depressed also, and, that, that was something they

shared in common. I broke down. I lost it, because I knew. I knew that

my best friend had just taken his life. That news hit hard.

It was about three weeks later that we got the truth and details

about what really took place. He sure enough did it. Joe Duke and his good friend, teamed up, drove off the cliff together just like Thelma & Louise,

and drowned. Tragically, his body was found 29 miles from where they

went in to the Colorado River. They were both unrecognizable. It took

dental records to get a positive ID. It is so hard, to find words, to describe

the feeling I had hearing about Joe Duke. I was depressed. There was

nothing I could do but think about the wonderful times I had with this

precious teenager. I, still today, embrace a large degree of love I had for

this person. I have to admit, I did not get over it over night. I was so

young. The resilience you have when you are growing up, I must say, I

took for granted, so, it amazes me that I pulled through. It was a lot

to overcome.

The advantage about being a human being is, that, we have handy

access to ways to overcome devastating losses, now days, more than ever.

We have to embrace it, and thank our lucky stars for what we do have.

I suppose we should feel lucky, to be in America.

Olla, attempted to make amends with Beth, and I after we

graduated from Durango. I had gone through four years of depression

during my summers there in Los Luna, before society became really

familiar with the seriousness of the blues. Most of my Hispanic and

Caucasian friends there, were living with parents driving fast cars and

motorcycles while I worked my skinny little ass off to pay my rent.

I can't tell you how liberating it was to graduate and move on. My good

friends were using my two room shack to party. I loved the company for

a while, but, the neighbor was furious with the noise. I eventually

got to the point when I had to communicate, to them, my frustration. I

had trouble getting across to them the grief and despair I began to suffer.

I really did love all those guys, that I went to school and partied with.

There for a while during my high school days in Los Luna, we

formed a small clan we called the family. As small as this little village was,

drugs of all sorts would snake their way in to town like heat waves.

Our little experimental family would all get together, drop acid (LSD) and

party from 24 to 48 hours. Vista Del Hombre, was 10 miles South. We

would drive there and hang out on the banks of the Rio Grand River. Just

about every time I would use LSD, I would feel like I had lived before, and

I knew ALL. I was actually counting my life backwards, and as time

progressed, I was unlearning, into regression. For a period, I felt

like I comprehended everything in the universe. This was around the

time Pink Floyd came out with 'Umaguma', and 'Obscured by Clouds.'

Jethro Tull came up with 'Aqualung.' These were extremely mind bending

times. We didn't leave anything out. We would use reds one week. Then mescalin, the next time. All the while, all of us were becoming serious

alcoholics.

Like I started to say, Olla, wanted to keep the peace with us

in 1972. She was living in Tulsa, the year I graduated, and, she met

the guy that was running for the state senator at a church she had been

attending. It turns out that this guy happened to have a ranch a few miles

south of town. She found out when meeting him that he needed an extra

hand plowing his wheat fields. I, was so broke and tired of the 'too much

of nothing' in my life back then. I agreed to give 'em a hand on that

ranch. Douglas Melrose. He turns out to be one of the most selfish mer-

chants I had run across, since I left Durango.

The rancher had several large tractors with a plow especially

designed to lift and drop a plow with hydraulics. It wasn't a bad job. I

worked 10 to 15 hours a day. They hired and fed another kid. The two of us shared a small bunker trailer. The only thing I hated about the driving

job was that they kept treating me like I was a mischievous ornery teen.

They did not trust me. One guy kept driving out to make sure I didn't

stop and take a nap. He kept checking my rows, and, I surprised them all

with, next to perfectly straight rows at the end of each day. I was in for a

surprise though, when it came to settling up, as the job ended.

This turned out to be a very interesting affair on this tractor job

the year of June of 1972. This job gave me the opportunity to reminisce a-

bout the many unbelievable and tragic events that when on in Los Luna.

It was good to get away from it all for a time, long enough, to repair some

of the hurt and forget the sorrow I had mounted over the past four years.

I was finally able to except I was not going to see, Joe Duke again. I was

also having to get used to being a reject & an outcast, having such an odd personality in high school. Every girl I attempted to get close to at Los

Luna high and, Durango, dumped me like a sack of trash. I got so used to

being rejected in my elementary and early school years that, this didn't

bother me near as much, as being a bully magnet and being targeted by

the violence. I guess I must have figured there was always going to be a lot

of fishes in the sea, but my self esteem was, still, in a lot of trouble.

Most importantly, I was not familiar with self esteem. If asked, I could not

have even defined the word. Durango, like a lot of schools back then were

just not taking the role, or reaching out the hand, so to speak, to really

prepare a kid for becoming successful, financially, and most important,

emotionally! With this cross I had to bear, I made some very bad

decisions at that tender age. Quite a few of my friends in Los Luna, were

also headed straight to an early grave yard. There was so much alcoholism and drug abuse, that, there was no escape when *the blues*

came to town.

The job outside of Hays City, came to an end in about six weeks,

and, there I was, on the last day of plowing. The foreman then ordered,

to fill the trucks to haul the wheat, then said, But... Doug ain't gonna pay

you little twerps for driving them wheat trucks. It didn't make sense. This

is where I got to see first hand how, the more some men have, the less

they are willing to share. This guy was a very successful wheat rancher.

He probably had 200 thousand bucks worth of farm equipment. Not to

mention he is now hauling the entire season of crops. He was worried

about over paying two homeless teenagers money for hauling the

wheat trucks. After working six weeks, the man pays us a little over two

hundred and ninety dollars.

Things got real interesting from that moment forth. This exchange of peanuts for six weeks of, sometimes, 15 hour days was to give

me a very odd perspective of understanding the exchange of the legal

tender. I was setting out on a journey of unbelievable, extreme

diversity. Like 'Little Big Man', I wasn't just carrying a 'cross'. I was to find

out how to take it back across the street and carve an instrument out of it.

The irony of my entire life was, that, I wasn't holding any major

animosity toward anyone I came into contact with, nor, did I plot or seek

revenge for any past attacks on me. Sometimes I wonder if I was really the

one doing the driving. I kept having dreams of being attacked by

one or several aggressors, and, not being able to move and fight back. All

of my life up to age 50, I dreamed this. Since then, for some reason, I

now dream of striking back, actually making contact and hurting the

attacker(s). I wake up now, after kicking or punching the wall that my bed is up against. There's been a couple of times I have thought I broke a bone

in my hand and/or foot. I've been fortunate. I should probably talk to a

shrink.

Since the boys ranch in Oklahoma, I have always had a guitar

around. There were large spaces after graduating high school, when I did

not carry one. I believe with all my heart that music is what saved my

my life. After doing some traveling and returning, I soon began to

learn song after song and taking music very seriously. The songs that

that appealed to me were not religious. The songs that were getting

through were melancholy, constructive, empathetic, and practical

master pieces of a higher way of thinking. 'BOB DYLAN' is the most

influential writer of the 21ˢᵗ century. He and the 'BEATLES' showed

people like me, how to crawl back to the threshold after falling off of

opportunity. When I left Hays City, I was more lost than after leaving

Durango, but, I sure was paying attention to the genius artwork of these

fine song writers. The approach that I took, as I wondered aimlessly

kept me in check, and, I had more of a tendency to sing than to fight.

The only thing I could think of, about where to go, to spend all of

this money I earned at the ranch, was to fly to Hawaii and pick pineapples

while they were in season that summer. I had met and hung with a

Japanese student teacher in my senior year there at Durango. We shared

some ideas in common, and, she liked a couple of the songs I had written

with the cheap guitar I had, that last year. She was raised in Hawaii and

flew back there soon after the 1972 class ended. We were half way

attracted to each other. After hitch hiking to Los Angeles, getting an a

air fare to the Island where she was, and, flying there, it turned out to be

a bad move. She had got back with her mean ole boyfriend, and, I ended up seeing her for a few minutes, before I split Hawaii. Disgustingly, I

chose to return to the U.S. after listening to all of her good friends. They

all kept telling me to fly back now if ya got the dough. The jobs paid

so little that they thought it would take month of Sundays' to earn an air

fare back. I took their word and flew back 2 days later. I got off the plane

and hitched back to New Mexico.

It must be surprising, to you young readers, to hear about

how someone could stick out their thumb and actually have cars stop for

you and travel across the states to go anywhere. This is how it was. It was

safe. People were different. It was a different world, and, I surely, was to

be one of the first 'desperados' to find out the hard way, the one con-

sistency. That would be, how quickly, things change in the United

States. Back then there was no such word as 'homeless'. I was a 'traveling

troubadour' with nothing else to offer but, the willingness to work, and, what I had to add to the central opinionated philosophy. Taking turns

at shooting at what we all thought made sense of the universe. If you saw

the movie, 'The Beach' that starred Leonardo DiCaprio, you would have an

idea of what kids were experiencing in the 70s. We were seeking what we

primarily, thought, was the second wave of the 'land of milk and honey,

the bible speaks about. People like me, were leaning in that color of

direction, because of the tremendous void, I had, coming from a *zero*

family, and, lack of stability.

I visited Beth and Derek, for a few days back in New Mexico. We

learned that our cherished mother had moved again. She was now in

Tulsa, Oklahoma. She did invite me to come to visit her there. I guess we

both wanted to give each other another chance at pooling our resources

and new found knowledge to get along. I tried so hard to live with Olla again there in Tulsa, but, she started her nagging again. She just wouldn't

leave God out of the picture. I couldn't do anything right. I had to

move on.

I met a guy who helped me get a job as a yardman at a Pepsi Cola

distribution facility. That company was paying me two dollars an hour

while I worked like an immigrant in the heat. I did get an apartment.

I figured out pretty quick that I got myself in a situation of going

absolutely nowhere at an incredible speed. Olla wasn't much help. Bless

her heart. She just wanted me to be happy. She just seemed to be

naturally drawn away from ways to make money, which is probably the

primary reason she fell into the fanaticism of religion in the first place.

She just couldn't and wouldn't network with anyone who seemed to be

attempting to make money. It was contradictive how she would say

that money was the root of all evil. Then, she would turn around and say that she would give anything to have a home in Hawaii with unlimited

resources. Again, this was terrible influence on Beth and me. I had to

make a decision. I had to make a change that would launch a brighter

future. I knew this was only going to happen through nobody's effort but

my own. So I did take a plunge.

After working a few weeks as a yardman, making a few friends

and learning the song 'Sundown' by Gordon Lightfoot, I went down to

talk to an army recruiter. He made a lot of promises and then threatened

me with the fact that my draft lottery number was very low, and, I was

going to be drafted and probably sent to Vietnam. I had talked to, two or

three friends in Los Luna, that had been there on a tour. They all related

well to me, and had me convinced, that it would be pretty stupid to join

or wait to get drafted. So, I joined and, reenlisted an additional year to be guaranteed to spend my first year in Korea.

Meanwhile, back in the hook of Los Luna, Beth, gave birth to

the most beautiful little boy, naming him Jacob. Just as fate would surely

have it, he turns out to be the most sane and successful one among us all.

He was smart. He, at least learned a trade, while in the military.

There was opportunity in those days to do anything. The market

was wide open. The competition was at a minimum. You could have sold

sunglasses to a blind man. I had three jobs in New Mexico. I had already

moved from the apartment Beth, and I first rented together. I rented

another little shack with Derek. He moved out while I worked at an Enco

gas station that was within walking distance, the summer of 1970. I had

dealings with everything from, Bikers to beautiful women, looking to get

laid. Life had not left much to my imagination. I had already experienced life in the fast lane, and shaking hands with the Devil. So, I needed a BIG

change. I needed more money, but, I had all the wrong reasons in mind

about what to do with money. I just wanted a car. I just needed a bump up

from this extreme poverty, to being able to have what the kids my age

had.

I could have made a much bigger difference in my economic pit

fall, if I would have known better than to join the army. I, of course, do

not regret my choices back then. Kids like me really needed to make

a big change. The military service was, unfortunately an uncomplica-

ted way off the street. So, I hopped on a bus to Fort Leonardwood, MO.

I went through basic training there and finished my advanced indidvi-

dual training in Fort Polk, Louisiana. Anyone that's been in the navy or

army knows, that if we all went into detail of the many experiences one has while serving, knows you could take up the next five chapters. So, I do

need to continue to cut to the chase while I still can.

Beth was smart. She remained in Los Luna, when I left the U.S.

Our dear ole Dad came to visit us for a third time after Beth, had

graduated from high school. He had a nice car, gave her a television and

tried to get her hooked up in college courses that would have been funded

by the government. Ansel, was rewarded an allotment to use for helping

families get through bettering their education. She chose to stay back on

home front, be a good mother and raise Jacob. Derek, probably had a hand

in that decision. I think she realized, down the road, that she could have

done both. We were not exactly versed in making the best decisions, back

in the day. I shouldn't need to remind my readers that we both were

surely lacking good business skills and decisions that involved our future

and fate.

After finishing all of my military training, I boarded an army air-

craft to Korea, I'll never forget stopping off to fuel in Japan. The airport

there filled up like a Chinese fire drill. I had never seen so many slant

eyed people gathered in one place on such a cold day, but, we were soon

back in the plane destined for a mind bending bunch of wild experiences.

Korea is a very different environment. Especially back in the 70s.

The country side was mostly rice patties and straw huts. I sobbed as we

rode in the back of the doose & a half covered personnel carrier. I remem-

ber becoming extremely depressed the day we drove up to the DMZ. My

first permanent duty station was Camp Pellam that stretched from the

freedom bridge to the JSA- Joint Security Area.

I was assigned to a mortar unit for my first six months. We went

on 18 hour patrols into North Korea. We carried live ammunition. But we never did exchange fire with the so-called enemy. I got along with the

Korean soldiers better than I did with the Americans, but, I was not

wowned up too tight like a lot of the higher ranking staff over me. My

platoon sergeant never did like me. I wound up being assigned

to the unit police. We guarded the six check point shacks that surrounded

Camp Pellam. I also guarded Freedom Bridge. The original was bombed

during the Korean conflict in the 60s. It had only one lane. We had to stop

traffic on the north end, while the south end passed through. I worked

twelve hour shifts at night. It wasn't difficult to stay awake. It was either

sub zero temperatures or summer infested mosquito company.

It may sound like tough duty, but, the patrols we went on, when I

was in the mortar platoon, was ten times worse. We would walk for hours

into the DMZ. Then we would sit for hours after sweating profusely. I would get cold. Some times, when we got back, there would be, little, or

no hot water in the latrine. I would be so dirty and needing to take a

shower that I would take one anyway when it was below freezing outside

the barracks. When I was re-assigned to the unit police, I really began

to actually like Korea. I began to come out of my depression after six

months of a cold hell and a Sergeant that treated me like I was bug that

needed to be squashed.

I'm going to attempt to tell you about the near by villages that we

all visited on our time off duty without taking up the next few chapters.

First of all, I saw right away that the Koreans were a very humble and a

tough bunch of people. I identified, up front, that if you treated most

of them with respect and as an equal, you had a true friend. Even the

hookers. They were the most precious and innocent bunch of peasants.

I could easily see why a lot of G.I. troops married Korean women.

Chamajuri, was the closest village to the DMZ. Korea was poverty

stricken in the 70s, and, just about everything you bought there would fall

apart within a few weeks to a year. If you bought a coat for example. The

thread they would use would not hold up to any degree of strain. The

albums of musical artists would play a couple of times and would soon

begin to skip. The material was uniform. But they had not mastered

quality and endurance. We all still bought many items from the villages.

We were not exactly in position to complain and take things back. After

all, everything *was* cheap. including the women. Guys would pay $1.25

for a short time, and $5.00, for all night sex with a prostitute. Most of the

girls did not really enjoy the intercourse. Some did. Some would try to rip

you off. I met one girl who would trade sex for buying toasters, blenders, silver ware, and what have you, from the American PX store with her

money. Her Mother trusted me. They knew I was not going to rip them

off. Those wonderful souls could see right through you. They had dealt

with enough jack-ass G.I.s to know a bad apple when confronted with one.

From what I hear, Korea has been fortunate enough to see a big

positive change since I was there. Several American companies have set

up business and factories and, have brought in bucket loads of jobs.

This poor country has finally exploded into a very prosperous and pro-

ductive country.

I rarely went to the villages with anyone. I usually went alone. It

was that safe back then. I began to realize that I was becoming more

and more uncomfortable around others. I suppose you could say that I

had been rejected so much in the past that I had, had it with superficial friendship, and, I sure had good reason to feel that way at Camp Pellam.

Some of the higher ranking soldiers were pretty gung ho. They saw me

coming, and, the last thing most of those guys would ever do would be

to extend a hand of friendship. Luckily, I did bond with several of the guys

at the U.P. outfit. I met a guy named Tori. He played guitar good.

We would hike up the mountainous hill behind our barracks next to the

bridge and play songs we both knew. We had a lot of fun with music.

There was a cute little lake about a hundred feet from our nest.

The villagers would sell ice skates for a dollar. They didn't fit so well.

The lake froze over, come November. We would smoke pot and have the

time of our lives with speed skates on that stupid little lake with our feet

hurting like hell. I never did find a pair of figure skates. The speed

skates we did find and use had not evolved long enough to meet the de-

mand, and to fit like they should, but, again, we didn't complain.

It was hard to believe, the contrast of the unit police life, verses

the infantry division, where I was, for the first 6 months. I had a suicide

idea all planned out just before they transferred me from the mortar

platoon, but, I was that way before I even landed on the DMZ. It seemed

like I just couldn't shake the black cloud that kept raining on my parade,

and, continued after I got out of Durango. All the while though, I may not

have welcomed it, but, I was becoming tough as leather. With the

open mind I had, I was also turning into a very flexible kid.

After about five months with the U.P.s, I took a leave and hopped

a train to Seoul. I found a cheap hotel, found a nice hooker, spent the

night, and, just about lost all my money. I had a big wad of American $20

dollar bills. One of the women that ran the place saw what I had. Later

that night she waited til she thought I went to slept. She then tip toed in the room and attempted to, not just try to get the bills, but she grabbed

my only pair of pants. She would have got me for everything I had, if I had

not been awake. Knowing me though, I didn't make a big stink. I simply

used my pants for pillow for the rest of the night.

I wish I had kept in touch with the troops I had developed such a

bond with, while at Camp Pellam. One of my roommates at the UPs was a

real good drummer. He would use a 5 gallon bucket with a set of drum

sticks and jam with my guitar. We jammed up a storm of blues, country,

rock-you name it. I just wish I had values like I have now. What I would

give, to get back in touch with these guys I knew back then on the DMZ.

I was so dumb when I joined the army. I just wanted to drive a

truck. After going through the process of enlisting and beginning to train,

we went through a permanent duty choice class. I was just glad I was not being shipped off to Viet Nam. Like I said, I had re-enlisted for a third

year to be guaranteed to spend my first duty station in Korea. I failed the

truck driving exam, and I let that man talk me in to making infantry my

M.O.S. Not realizing I had a better choice than what he was offering, I

could have insisted on being given the chance to study with a second

crack at testing and passing the truck driving test. I was so aimless and

confused. You can see why a teenager is going to be feeling alone

hopeless and depressed being dropped off at the DMZ.

I was in Korea for just a few weeks when the Vietnam war finally

came to an end in 1973. I do cherish my tour in Korea. Any overseas duty

in the military is going to be an unforgetable experience. I came to

love every minute of it towards the end of my thirteen month duty time

there. Even the food was unusually good after you acquired a taste for it.

You could smell kim-chi,as soon as, you stepped off the airplane, arriving in that area of Korea.

If I had, had a choice after leaving Korea, I would have extended

my time in the army just to spend it back in Korea. I randomly chose

Fort Hood, Texas to finish my three year enlistment. Let me tell ya,

brothers and sisters, that was a very bad choice. Fort Hood was not a hell

hole like, maybe, getting stuck in a military operation in Alaska, but, by

this time I had realized that I did not really want to be a soldier in the

Army, in that capacity. I did not relish the idea that, I, at any time could

be among others to be deployed and sent off to the middle east or back to

the orient to fight. Our daily formations, always brought something new.

Just to renew my faith, the platoon sergeant announced, the next

day, that, we were all gonna go on a military exercise in Germany. After

adjusting to that idea, we had one week to prepare to get ready to deploy to Europe, to carry out a field training mission there called, Re-forger.

Germany was different, very green, but the locals were friendly.

I was elected to drive the scout front convoy jeep, with the Alfa

warrant officer. We were in the field the whole 45 days we were there.

I'll never forget the intense woods, with deer stands, every half mile.

You would be in the middle of nowhere, and out of somewhere, a German

couple, holding hands would show up, walking through a leisure time in

the forest. This blew my mind. I envied, and admired them. Several times,

when driving by, in open tanks, A.P.C.s and jeeps, the German children

would run up and drop a bunch of, very tasty, fresh grapes and apples in

our lap. The kids loved the G.I.s. We would also, put the locals to work.

They would literally, get a kick, out of throwing delicious apples at us

goof ball soldiers when we were high up on the tanks and trucks.

One night, the brigade officer, brought a large amount of great

German beer. We all got our fill, and had a great time. I had been getting

headaches a few months before that time. Out of nowhere, I found out I

was a victim of my mom's condition. I unfortunately, discovered just how

bad the genetic pull, was affecting me, that night. The next day, my head

hurt so bad that, I took off into the forest alone in a state of confusion.

I ended up digging a hole, taking an allergy pill with some excedrin. I then

buried myself in that hole and slept. Waking up, I panicked, thinking

the whole brigade had expired their time at that location, and left. I ran

back to the camp and, the warrant officer, was going nuts, accusing me

of going a.w.o.l. He must have liked me, because, he kept me for a driver

and never pressed charges. We finished the tour together, and, I found

myself, facing a new life with uncontrollable headaches. I loved to drink beer, but, found it, to surely be a trigger for bad migraines. German beer

was like drinking fire on the mountain, for me.

For years after that, I would find myself spending sometimes

24 to 48 hours in and out of bed, with migraine headaches. The con-

dition, would really zap my ambition. I later learned, by 1999, that

the FDA finally approved Imitrex/Sumatriptan. An ole man in Arizona

was nice enough to let me try it. By the grace of luck, and technology, I,

for the first time in 35 years, got rid of a serious headache. Unfor-

tunately, my poor mother, Olla was killed before she, and a lot of healthy

migrainers, ever got a hold of Imitrex.

By this time, Olla, had moved from Tulsa, OK to Garland, Texas.

She lived in Plainview for a while. By the time I had returned from

Korea, she had already moved 5 or 6 times, which was not surprising. She

was about 165 miles from Fort Hood. I traveled back and forth every once a month to visit her there in Garland. I had taken out an allotment for

her to aide her while I was in the army. It discontinued when I was

discharged in 1975. This was another reason we all would have been

better off, if I would have stayed in for at least 20 years. Those days,

I have to tell you, were very different. The whole economy structure was

nothing like it is today. There wasn't a quarter of the merchandise in

stores, back then, that we have today. The things that we have to buy with

money now, out weighs the gismos a thousand to one back in those days.

I left the service mainly to keep my sanity. It wouldn't have

made a lot of sense to remain in an army as a C.O. I just wanted out.

Today, you can imagine how I feel, realizing my mothers' allotment

funds were cut off. We can't save the world, but, if you have the chance

to help a family member, jump on it. You will never forgive yourself when

the day comes along when you realize that it hurt them badly
because

you did not show much love and consideration in their time of
need. Give

it some time to think about consequences when making financial
choices

involving family.

   I had been renting an apartment off base in Sandeau the
last few

months before I was discharged in September '75. The landlord
happened

to be a friend of the gal that was renting property to my mom in
Garland

while I was still in the service. I was offered a room, rent free, in
another

large house in exchange for collecting rent money from the
tenants each

month that lived in the 4 additional apartments there in Sandeau.
I was

to remain in the bed room, and I was not granted access to the
rest of the

house, and that was fine. It was a spooky place anyway. I was
not real

comfortable in that place, but, to top things off, I was soon to get
a good,

long lasting taste of serious horror. The kind of terror that I was very un-

familiar with, was, just about to send me off the deep end.

Jane Cross, and, Peter, were two people I met, and, was hanging

out with while living in Sandeau. I think I met Peter through one of my

army buddies that I initially befriended on base at Fort Hood, named

Arin, Arin and Peter were both bi/gay. I remember walking in

on their lust affair a couple of times. Peter was interested in me, but, I

really did not have any attraction for the same sex, and, I felt badly for

Arin. He had an insecurity that I knew I could not do much about. He

was so attracted to me, that, it was uncomfortable.

I don't remember how or where I met Jane, but, I found out one

night just how much she liked sex. I was soon to find this out, but,

the circumstance I am about to share with you, I must say, has got some

kind of twist!

These two people came over to the place I was care taking back in

June of the year I was discharged. Joy asked me if I had seen or heard a-

bout 'The Exorcist'. At that point in my life, I didn't even know what

Exorcist meant. She explained to me a little about it, but, I think they

pretty much expected me to know it's meaning. They both assumed that I

knew more about it. Joy didn't even say, that, it was a horror movie.

We got to the theater, and, looked around in the pitch dark

to find that the only seats that left were the front row. This was the first

time in my life that I was left with no choice, but, to take a chair that

was right up against the enormous screen. The theater was packed, so,

I figured it must really be worth seeing.

The movie, I thought, began with an interesting story there in

Iraq. If you have seen the 'Exorcist', you will know what I mean when I

say: *"shock."* I was OK until Reagan drastically changed. I walked out afterwards not really feeling that affected. The three of us went

back to my place and drank wine 'til we were all pretty stupid. Before you

knew it, we all ended up in a threesome. Peter became very distraught

after I did not really include him. He joined in uninvited assuming I would

take on a bi-role. The importance of the evening that, I tried to balance

here, is,that the experience I had when we all composed ourselves and,

they went on home. The back of the house I was caretaking was, just, ex-

tremely dark. It was so quiet. All I could see and, think about was

that little girl that changed into the scariest figure I had ever seen. Hell,

I was still half drunk, but, I was so freaked out, that, even after turning

all the lights on, I ended up taking a sheet & pillow and crawling into the

cab of my truck. I finally got a couple hours sleep. Every night after that,

I would either end up in the truck, or at Jane's house. I never did see anything in that darkness, really. The house, actually had a very clear and

safe aura. I should say, that, I felt relieved that there really wasn't

anything to be concerned about as far as the house having a past. You

could have *never* convinced me back then, that, that house, was free of

any haunting activity.

Jane and I, continued to date and had a lot of great fun together.

Peter, continued to have fun in the sack with Arin, and, a couple of

months later I finally got out of the army. The incidents, and all the

shocking scenarios, I took with me, like a new skin clinging to my body as

if I were made out of honey.

The first project I began working on was building a camper for

the back of the 1966 Chevy pick-up. I had traded my Ford Maverick for

the truck. I took quite a loss when I did that, because, I overhauled the

6 cylinder engine out, in the barracks parking lot, by myself about seven

months, into my time, there at Fort Hood. I failed to clean the pistons

correctly, and, I ended up taking it to a mechanic who tore it all down a-

gain, cleaned the pistons, and put it all back together, for $160 bucks! He

was so fair. I could not believe, that someone in his position would do

that much work and, charge so little. I surely poured out my gratitude

to that guy. He was a jewel.

I got started on building the camper at Olla's rented property

next to her apartment. I built the frame using 2x4s when I should have

used 1x4s. It ended up being very heavy. I could sure sleep back there. It

was typical of me to come up with a house on wheels because, I sure did

continue to ramble and go everywhere once being freed from the bondage

and stronghold of the military. I was so happy to get out, it was pathetic!

I was still so stupid. All I thought about was letting my hair grow and try living as far from the walls of society as possible-not realizing how de-

pendent I was on money. So went, the influence, I victimized myself with.

Oh man, the world was so different then. Unless you had a good friend

or a merchant parent, to show you that, money is, in the end, the thing

that is going to be, what really, turns the key, you got lost those days.

I finished the camper and left my poor mother to support herself.

I just didn't think much, back then, about her situation. She no longer

would receive the allotment, and, I could not wait to get down the road

far away from her. She was really alone. She never remarried. It didn't

affect me much back then. I not only had a lot of growing up to do & we

just could never be friends. I find that so sad now that I have grown older.

The religion really took a toll on our small family. She just kept pushing

us away. Beth, and I wanted so badly to be closer to her, but the

Pentecostal influence she was succumbed by, was really, what drove the

wedge between us. To this day, I will never stop wishing it could

gone down differently. I loved my mother a lot more than I thought I did.

She made it so hard for us to know how to express that.

The first thing I wanted to do was visit Beth in Los Luna. She

remained in that sweet little hell hole, the whole time, I was in the army. I

did have a surprisingly soft place in my heart after all, and I took my

mother, Olla, with me to visit Beth, in New Mexico. I was so hooked on

the alcohol and the drugs that flowed into Los Luna, and, here I was

bringing our religious mother with me. Looking back into, and writing

about how I grew up, it would not be out of line to say that everything I

ate, carried, lusted for, moved, challenged, worked for, lived for, voted

for, used, abused, fought for, extracted, employed, deployed, ran toward and ran away from, was all extreme. Olla, had a whole lot, to do with

that. I'm finding these days that some people, not only, don't believe

me, but, some can't handle the conversation. They are either envious,

jealous, or they have been so sheltered all their lives, that, they are

completely offended when I share just one or two of my scenarios. I say

Olla, had everything to do with it, because she moved us so often, into

so many extreme situations. Then, I ended up in the army, too stupid to

stay in the army, and, learn a skill or a trade.

Olla, was happy to see Beth. She stayed a few days and went on

back to Dallas. For the first time in her life she remained in the suburb of

Garland there for the last 20 years that she lived. I was happy to be out of

the military and around family. It was to be one of our last times the

three of us would all be together.

For that time being, I remained inside the hook of Los Luna. I got an apartment right across the street from where Beth, and I had

rented the shack during high school. It was where I lived when being

kicked out of high school in Los Luna. I invited my army buddy, Jake, to

split the rent and live with me there until we decided what direction life

would continue to point us to. I found myself having to make decisions

based on where I could find peace and quiet, and still have fun with

friends and family. I did begin to value a better kind of income.

I was so much in the habit of moving and uprooting,that, I

I ended up moving into a garage in Frog Valley. I joined the mosquito's

next to the beautiful run off creek. It was quiet and solitary. I needed

peace of mind, badly. I at least was out from under the cloud of a crowd

of bullies, and, for once I had found a haven of rest.

I must have stayed in the Jansen's Garage every bit of six weeks,

when, Rocky Zantano, stopped in for a visit. He lived in a trailer close by. I went back with him to his place that day to find a stranger

resting on his couch. I saw this very strong looking figure stretched out

there, not looking very lazy, or relaxed. I asked Rocky who it was, as he

invited me in. It was the first time I ever saw Daniel, from up North.

I had so much love and admiration for Rocky, and his partner, Rose.

I really valued the time that I got to visit these two absolutely creative

hip, intelligent and interesting people. I did feel a bit inferior around

them those days, but they didn't ever attempt to make me feel stupid

or unwanted. They introduced me to Daniel. This guy is, mister Cool.

Daniel, had an aura about him that stopped you in your tracks. You just

couldn't help, but be drawn in. He did what he could to, *not* make you

feel inferior. I felt like I could never measure up to this guy. He did take a liking to me. We hung out there in Los Luna for a few days. Daniel, was

traveling through New Mexico, on his way to Houston. He had a brother

there, and Daniel, would stop off on his way to the Yucatan. He had been

traveling down there just about every year while he was in his twenties,

back when Mexico was safe, safe enough for a Gringo to travel alone, or,

with another guy, without being attacked or kidnapped for ransom.

Daniel, was either full of beans, or just plain lonely when he in-

vited *me*, to journey with him all the way to Costa Rica. I said Mooahhh?!!!

You have got to be kidding. He eventually convinced me that he was sin-

cere. I was elated to except his offer, not thinking about the fact that I had

basically no money saved at that time. He assured me that we could raise

the money needed in Texas.

The dog I had, there at Beth's house, named Rusty, just gave birth to a litter of 6 pups. Beth insisted I take them with me. Let me tell

ya brother, that was a big mistake. I piled them up under the front seat of

the pick-up cab. We drove those poor dogs all the way to Austin, before

we realized we really needed to find homes or drop them at the ASPCA.

I mapped it out and, I found a shelter that Texas town. We kept two

pups, and the mother.

Arriving in, Houston the 2nd day, was a challenge. I had never seen,

nor drove in that kind of traffic. It seemed like people were driving like

there was no tomorrow. We finally got to Daniel's brother's apartment.

I felt like an imposition bringing three dogs with me. His brother, Jess,

I thought, really had his shit together. I couldn't help but admire

this guy. He was transporting new vehicles' in a tractor trailer, making

over $7oo a week. That was good money for an uneducated trade back

then. He had an OK place there in Houston. It was small and upstairs.

Not the best place for 3 dogs.

Wayne had a girlfriend there close by that agreed to care for the

mother dog I had. She also lent me $300 for our trip to Central America.

That doesn't sound like much, but, it was enough to fly to Merida and take

the cheap buses' to the Caribbean coast. I found that I had to stretch the

little money I borrowed, even though it a long way. I later caught myself

wondering throughout the trip, why I even tagged along, several times.

Daniel is from a cattle ranch. He did have empathy for me, but, it became

clear shortly after our arrival in Costa Rica that I should take my

remaining $130 bucks and fly back to the U.S, before I ran out of funds

altogether. When we are young we just don't take into account that we all

need to prepare ourselves for a historical journey of such a magnitude. I

was so ignorant, but, I had already hitch hiked to California before I even graduated high school. So I had been used to traveling with little or no

money, and, Mexico fit right into my level of stability. I would have

never been able to live with myself if I would have said no to the trip and

opportunity. Daniel, never said, he was going to pay my way. We were

both so young and, so full of it... it was funny.

After arriving in Merida at night, I was so excited, that, we never

did sleep until we reached the coast. The buses in South Mexico, back

then, were dirt cheap, and, we continued the next day to hitch and ride

for next to nothing. We were elated, and, it was around that point of the

trip that, after getting on a bus several times, that, I couldn't help but

notice something real special. There were so many women and children

riding to their destinations, that, many times they had to stand, hanging

on for dear life. The drivers were insane! With the empathy I had developed up to that point, I found myself giving up my seat for them to

ride a little more comfortably. This is when I came up with the first few

lyrics to a song that I named right away. There couldn't have been a more

fitting, and, related name than: 'Trail to Costa Rica'. Daniel, and I had a lot

of fun with that song. We found humorous ways to compliment the guitar

work. It was a serious subject, and, I came up with a fairly decent recor-

ding of the song years later.

Isla Mujeres was one of the first Islands we visited. I probably had

more fun, relaxed time, and, lasting memories than any other tourist spot

during the whole trip. We rented a motel room, and, the next day the

owner of the place we stayed, took us out on his motor boat, and, taught

us how to spear fish! I got so worked up and inspired. I got such a kick out

of being able to load an arrow in a spring loaded spear-gun and, chase fish, shoot 'em, and take 'em home without ever using any fishing gear.

The first time I went into the water test my skills, I realized my partial

front teeth would not stay in when I put on the scuba mask. I asked this

guys' daughter that, tagged along, if she would hold on to my teeth while

I chased fish. When she refused, I didn't blame her. I spent that day

remembering the time I lost my teeth in an accident. It all flashed back to

when I went to visit my uncle Warren in San Jose, California. I hitched out

there when I was sixteen to look for a better job that I had in Los Luna.

After being picked up by a guy there that, in deed was able to put me

to work in landscape, I drove to Camden one day to visit Warren. I had

never met the guy. It was a shock for him. He seemed like an OK guy, and

he owned an auto parts store. I went back and lived with my friend in

San Jose for a few more weeks. That next year, Warren talked to Olla in

Los Luna, while I was about to enter into my high school senior year. I

don't know if mom asked him or if he offered, but I ended up on the bus

to live with Warren for my Senior Year. I got a job at a place called Prune-

Yard Shell gas station. I was on my bike one night on my way back to

Warren's. When I passed by the school I saw a couple of kids I had met

that were selling me pot. This time they had something else to smoke.

They asked me if I wanted to smoke some 'angel dust.' I, of course, agreed

with curiosity. I took approximately four hits-not knowing, nor did they

warn me, that, one hit was more than enough. All I can remember is

diving at the asphalt and bragging that it was OK to go there, and, that I

could tolerate the rocky water. A couple of hours later I woke looking up

from the concrete full of blood. I finally composed myself and found all

these guys cared about, was, worrying about getting popped by the cops for giving me something that knocked me out. We were all just kids. None

of us had much of a sense of what to do in general. I got up and went on

back that night straight to bed. The next day, the only story I could think

of to tell Warren, why I was missing all of my front teeth, was dumb. I told

him, and, his impatient wife that I got hit by a car. Big mistake. He called

the cops. A man came out for a police report, but, neither of them

believed my story. Later I thought that telling them I hit a tree branch

would have gone over much better. Warren, took me for a ride later to let

me know that everything he does was for himself. He was violently telling

me he is kicking me out, that I was a good for nothin' and in his way.

I did get my mouth taken care of by a dentist who issued me a

partial for the three front teeth. Before I could sneeze, though, I was back

on a bus. to Los Luna.

Daniel, did spear a fish that day, and I managed to hold on to my

teeth while I chased the same fish the whole time, as he made a fool out

of me, and got away. I wanted to try again the next day, but Daniel,

wanted to move on down the road, and we caught a ride with a guy in a

pick-up, that took us to Tulum.

I had never visited a ruins. Tulum is right on the coast line just a

few feet from the water. We spent the night there by the ocean and

headed south the next day. The buses ran down right through an area

where we could see Cancun from the shore. We heard it is very com-

mercialized. Daniel, suggested we could spend too much money there.

I'll always remember the night before I woke up with a stomach

bug. Daniel, brought his flute along and, we had the time of our lives

singing songs and making noise with a cool breeze off the water. We didn't even need to build a fire. It seemed like the moon was real close.

The next day, I believe I got anemic dysentery from perhaps a

soda bottle-who knows. It was at least two miles to the nearest road

headed South. I walked quite a ways feeling like I was going to fall over

dead, and, that is almost what happened. Daniel, really got a kick out

of the way I fell to my knees. Then, I laid down, puking my brains out. I

later composed myself and was able to get back up and walk to the road.

We got lucky. It was either the first or second vehicle that stopped to give

us a ride that, an American, happened to have an antidote. I got a rapid

relief shortly after taking it, but, I, of course was in my 20s. I was

fairly resilient. I had to be. Keeping up with Daniel, was a challenge.

Sometimes, it was like trying to keep up with a wildebeest.

We continued to hitch rides and ride the cheap buses through

Mexico into Belize. Just after we attempted to cross that border, a guard there thought I looked like a threat to Belize, I guess. He must have

associated me with someone trying to smuggle drugs. We went back and

found a kid, that, had a garage we slept in. He also had a remedy for the

dysentery I had. It rained so hard that night, I kept waking up and

checking the floor, for flooding. It cleared up the next day, and, you

should have seen the look of excitement on that child's face when Daniel,

presented him with a frisby. He borrowed some scissors that night to trim

my beard and hair. We waited for the changing of the guards, and, we

got through the border the next day.

Even back then, Belize was a great refuge and a very relaxed, kick

back, interesting place full of friendly locals. They actually welcomed us,

surprisingly. We looked like a couple of free loaders, and, as much of an

idiot that I was back then, I surely would have never done anything to

hurt any one of those people. They villagers were all so sweet and accommodating.

Daniel, had been to that area several times and knew to catch

a flight from Belize to Honduras. It saved a lot of time and wear and

tear on us. As we were descending, even a mile up, all you could see was

banana plantations from horizon to horizon. Honduras is genuinely an

extremely beautiful and productive country. As we walked from the

airport, to, and through the main streets South, we were surrounded also,

by orange trees. The oranges were literally free for the picking. Wind

falls were everywhere. I got such a kick out of this little old lady with a

cart full, selling oranges. I felt badly for her. I gave her a couple of bucks.

It reminded me of the movie 'Born in East LA' when Cheech gave this lady

with kids his entire merchant cart of oranges. He later was being chased

by some hateful thugs. The lady he gave the cart to, bomb barded the thugs with the oranges to help Cheech escape their wrath.

We soon hopped a bus that took us through the rest of Honduras

and into Nicaragua. The first thing I noticed was a volcanic peak in the far

distance. It was gorgeous, and, obviously semi-active as you could see

a cloud of steam floating upward. We continued to pass by two more

volcanic mountains on the road we were on there.

The most memorable events were probably when we got to

witness the amazing trip through the two countries and saw the sugar

cane process. It all began with the field workers, making very little money

hand cutting the cane. Others then, loaded it into small trucks. What

we saw, was, the vast number of all these little ½ ton trucks lined up in a

chain that must'a stretched over a mile, all waiting for probably hours to

deliver their single load, probably not more than one, to, two loads a day.

I thought to my self that day, my gosh, am I ever glad I am an American.

We eventually made it to Costa Rica. Daniel, managed to get a

hold of his friend, he had met there before. Other than that, I began

wondering why I had even continued to tag along with the small amount

of dinero I brought with me. Daniel too, was growing tired by this

time, himself. He wanted to hang with his friends and visit another

couple of hot spots there in San Jose. He suggested I use the remainder of

the few bucks I had left to board a flight back to Houston alone. I guess,

at that point, I realized for sure I was ultimately alone on this journey.

I took his advise, and, did catch a plane back. The only direct flight went

to New Orleans at that time. I'll never forget how good it felt when I

set foot on to American soil, even though I had to walk out and hitch hike

back to Houston.

In spite of poor planning, lack of sufficient funds and getting sick during the trip, I felt real good. I walked for miles through the

broncs of New Orleans. I was lucky I didn't get jumped. It was a very eye

opening time for me. Just before I walked through the down town area

of Marti Gras city, I happened along a run down vacant house. Right in

the front yard was pile of trash in the shape of pyramid, and, scattered

amongst the waste, was five dead pups. I walked up closer to find the

mother also deceased. They were the most beautilful great dane dogs

I had ever seen. It made me think about how my dog was there in Houston

waiting for me. After inching my way through New Orleans and

managing to get rides from there on into Houston, I was in for another

surprise that would make me wonder why I ever excepted Daniel's in-

vite to join him on such a journey. I felt so badly for the pups and mother

dog that I came across on my way back. That was a sight to behold. It was the kind of seen a person can only forgive the people responsible. Who

knows? Sometimes animals are better off snuffed, than, to suffer, not

having a caring owner. I just couldn't wait to get back to my dog in

Houston.

I ended up on the out skirts and riding buses back to Daniel's

brothers' apartment. Jess, was home when I did arrived, and was there,

scraping up the pups' feces in the kitchen. I, again, felt stupid bringing

that litter of dogs with me before we went to Central America. That

decision to do that would continue to bite me even harder in the ass, than

I ever dreamed. Shortly after Daniel, also returned, I got all excited about

heading over to Daniel girlfriends place to pick up my dog. When I got

there, she explained that, the responsibility of caring for Rusty became

more than what she wanted to deal with, understandably so. She lived in an apartment, and, the dog did mess up her place. She found a friend that

agreed to take the dog out to a better environment at a trailer court, but,

when I went out to pick Rusty up, she had jumped the fence and ran off. I

looked for her everywhere. She was just gone. It reminded me of losing

the dog I had when I was ten. We had moved temporarily and Sammy was

shot, being mistaken for a fox while a couple from the church were

allowing the dog to stay on their farm, out side of Mohave, NM.

I found myself having a difficult time with the loss. I just did

not realize just how attached I was. I really loved both dogs. I suppose

you could say I was just as callused about loss, as I was attached. We, can't

afford to play a blame game or carry grief. Even though I spent a life

time regretting a lot of decisions that turned out badly, I have found that

it is only adding to what I need to shake to hold on to my sanity. I say that because, I have not had a lot of advice in making choices and chosing the

one that is going to turn out right every time. Making selections, and

going with that choice, is all a part of our growth, and, I have surely

learned and tried to remember, the first time.

I got a job in Houston working as an oiler, on a drag-line cat. I

assisted a guy that was carving out a 100 foot wide flood control ditch.

It was a long drive to the job site, and, I slept in my camper on the back of

that truck, Daniel named, 'Blue'. I parked next to a creek that was full of

snakes and aquatic turtles. I would get up at night, to urinate, with a flash

light only, for fear of so many critters. I never did get bit, and, I always

slept so well after working on that machine.

The money I borrowed from Jennie amounted to, every bit of

350 bucks. I had earned around six hundred when I decided to leave

Houston. I wasn't really interested in learning to drive the Drag Line, but it was a good experience. I paid Jennie back, and I headed back to New

Mexico.

The Los Luna Hook, had a hold of a lot of people, including

Daniel. Hell, he could have by-passed that little ghost town, and, been

better off going through Colorado and Wyoming. Rocky, really, was

originally the reason, Daniel, even knew about Los Luna. I have to

admit that, I, felt more kinship and love there than any where else I have

lived, and, that is saying a lot. Rocky, first met Daniel, in Montana.

I guess it must have been 3 weeks later that, Daniel came back

through our little town. He, surprisingly had Jennie with him. Just

after hanging with us all for a spell, Daniel, invited me to ride along with

him and Jennie, back to his ranch in Montana. He got tired of Houston

pretty quick too. Soon the three of us were headed North.

After packing in a few things, like a tooth brush and a couple of

shirts, pants and a little food, I, joined Daniel, once again on a crazy aimless journey. He was headed home, but not me.

I was so addicted to travel those days in my 20s. Like I said,

you never heard the word 'Homeless' in the 60s, 70s nor the 80s. I was

taking advantage of the freedom that was so prominent. The world was

so different, and, being so young, I could virtually put everything I would

need in a small back-pack. I didn't even use excedrin or coffee. I had no

particulars. It's hard to believe, what the body can get by with, when you

are in your 20s. I was more bent on travel and exploration than most

people. I couldn't comprehend how someone would work all year, day

after day, and then, only take a 1 to two week vacation. That seemed so

impossible. I had become such a habitual drinker and smoker, that,

when someone would say something like: "I know this guy across town

who has a lot to share, and, is really a cool guy, but he does not drink or smoke". I would not want anything to do with him. I could not imagine

living in this world without the booze and tobacco. I was already an

alcoholic by age 15, and, that was not good for making any career or

financial decisions and choices.

So, there I was, again, on the road with Daniel. We drove through

Utah and Wyoming. I asked him, to drop me off in Idaho. I caught

rides back south into Utah. Little did I know, that, I was just about to

meet some people that would forever have a tremendous impact on my

aim, for the next few years.

I had just stopped in a 7/11 for a beer and peanuts, when I headed

south, just outside of Salina, Utah. I stood there for just a few short

minutes, when, a large brown bus stopped. The bus door opens up, and,

all I saw was this big red Irish setter greeting me at the steps. He stood

in the way so much, that, I struggled forever trying to get by and take a seat. The driver was a tall thin guy with waist length blonde hair. He

introduced himself as Charlie, and, the girl he had with him at the time

was Bana, both from Oregon. I did have my guitar with me. She

wanted me to play some songs, while I was so road-beat-tired. All I

wanted to do was sleep. That night I met the rest of the convoy. Behind

Charlie, was, another bus they called 'Sky Blue'. Both buses had Tipi poles

tied secure to the top rack. That night I got to meet the driver of the

second bus. Her name was Dawn. This gal was gorgeous. She was a

single mother of the two kids, she had with her. Arla, was around 14, and

her younger brother, Zabi, was very young-probably eight or nine. The

little guy was full of life. He was a happy kid, with a lot of energy.

We continued South that day, and, that night the crew of the

three vehicles camped next to a Utah spring. We had a fire, and, I played a bunch of Jackson Browne, Moody Blues and Dylan songs they all loved.

The next day, I met Jimi & Salina. They drove the 3rd car. These four

precious people would later turn out to have a tremendous impact on

my life. To put it lightly, this whole band of Gypsies greatly affected my

aim and which road I took from that day on. Jimi's alternator went out.

We got the part, and, I installed it myself. They all stepped back and

realized, I was good for somethin', and, began to develop a value for the

hitch hiker they picked up. The third morning I got up, said goodbye,

and headed down the road with my thumb stuck out. I did not have

as much regard for the convoy of freedom seekers, but, Salina got into

the small car with Dawn, and they drove up along side and proclaimed

that I was not to leave this abruptly at this time. I was impressed with their values. For the first time in my life, these people were tracking me

down to hold on to me, instead of rejecting me, and, looking for a place

to dump me off.

It took me a while to figure out what this group wanted, what

they were after and where they were really going. They were all so

personable and warm. There were four children along, and, all of them

were so polite and mature for their age. For once, I felt like I really met

some friends that were worth while hanging with.

The experience I had driving tractors, and, all kinds of vehicles

while I was in the army, proved to be an asset on my part. I was glad to

be considered a reliable relief driver, but, I had trouble believing that

their plan, was to homestead, in Mexico. After looking into getting

everyone across the border, they ran into couple of unexpected set backs

when trying to get through the border. Back then, for some reason, children had to have a certain kind of visa, and, with the time and money

involved, they all decided that it was not worth the trouble.

Jimi, was familiar with the area south of Tucson, and, he had

lived at a place called 'The California Fountain', so, we all headed in that

direction in the Spring of 1977. I thought this life style was, indeed, the

greatest adventure. The crew continued to be rational and determined

to survive the elements. Needless to say, they were intending to live

free of the system, and, try to be as independent of society as they could.

At the time this all sounded so unique and do-able. It is a very rough

terrain down there, and the road was next to impossible. I was surprised

to see the two old buses make it to the living area. The only thing, really,

that made the place any where near productive enough to be considered

a commune establishment was, that, there is a, 'well' there. I remember, that, the water did not really taste that good, but, up to that point, I had

never tasted reverse osmosis.

I overlooked a lot of attributes about 'The Fountain,' and, I loved

it there, because I felt loved. There was a kind of peace and harmony

along, with little prejudice. I was so taken by the new experience, that, I

told them "I'll be right Back." I got back out on the road and

hitched all the way back to Los Luna to pick up my pickup camper. I

told Beth, that I had found a new life, and, I'm goin' right back to Arizona

to live. I must have sounded totally lost, but, I was sold on my new life.

Beth was stuck. She had responsibilities, different than me. She,

at least, stood her own ground and did the best she could raising Jacob.

I remember Beth, before she moved from the trailer, that, she and Derek

lived in for a few months. She had always been a very shy, introverted, creative, smart, and a caring, nice person. They had found a home to

buy around the time I got out of the army, that proved to be another

reason to drive on and continue to thrive and survive. We would soon

find, we were all bloody victims. Even Daniel, kept coming back through,

Los Luna for few days, on his way back to Mexico. Jake, his brother,

Sebastian, and, many other friends would try living somewhere else,

seeking better employment, and, lo & behold, before you could even

remember them leaving, they would be right back. They would usually

find work right away in this odd little crazy town.

    I don't want to sound superstitious, but our aims began to change

when Beth and Derek, tried to make their lives better. Things started

to slip. I have spent a lifetime attempting to unravel and define why we

were all, so compassionate and loving and spending quality time, together. Then later, some of us finding fault in each other, after we had

been so close, for decades. I suppose we were all just a bunch of pathetic,

repeat victims, of the Los Luna hook.

7

TERROR ON SANTONA

Derek and I, had gone out east of town several times to get fire

wood. They had a cook stove there in the two story place they felt lucky

to purchase. We all really enjoyed the smell and the privilege of

being able to find, cut and haul our own fire wood. We went out to an

open range, that, to this day, I don't even know if any one owned the land

where we found our firewood. I would always remind Derek that, "Hello"

"We don't have a spare tire on the truck," and, he would say "Don't worry

about it." I would say, "Well if you asked me...I---" and, he would say:

"Well nobody asked you." There we were, every time, going miles out

of town to the middle of Ten-Buck-Two-nowhere, without, a spare tire!

I had been spending quite a bit of time with Beth, at their new

place after getting out of the army. The house was made of stone, put

together with concrete. It had a very nice screened in front porch that

faced the street. I guess the original owner deemed it necessary to add an

add on. He did a make shift attempt of creating a kitchen and a 2nd bath-

room. The kind of quality that would have never passed code inspection.

It worked OK as a make shift partial and 2nd bathroom.

The house sits on the corner of Santona and second avenue just

a few steps from the down town area to the East. The Rio Grand River

was with in walking distance, West of the property. I guess you could say

this house was the first living space that Beth and I, ever occupied that presented itself with something beside a fly-by-night temporary dwelling.

We just never had felt or experienced any kind of lasting security. I

didn't really think about, that, maybe, I was imposing on my sister. I was

young. I find it hard to believe how much I took for granted those days,

looking back. Growing up without the love we needed, so desparately

from caring parents, I must say, we were definitely a miss! I guess

I regarded my sister, to some degree, a parent figure, so to speak.

I was, so compelled, by the drop of the hat. One day I decided to

hitch to Kentucky to visit our Grand Mother. I went there one time while

Olla, was there alone with her. Other times I would hitch back out to

California. These episodes went on for years. Before I met Hopi & friends,

I had already hitch hiked to Kentucky twice. I hit California three or

four times. I had also visited Tennessee after finding out about 'the Farm'

and three other Communes of the 70s era. All-the -while, Beth, did remain at the house on Santona.

I suppose you could say, if I were to be asked if I believed in

ghosts at that time in my life, I would have, had, to say no. It would have

probably been the same, if you would have asked me about UFOs. We

didn't have much access to eye witness accounts about the paranormal

in books or television in the 70s. If Jacob would have told me back

then, that, he noticed the mountable rocking horse moving back and

forth by itself, then, sometimes, moving across the room closer to his bed,

I would have laughed, and, thought Jacob was making it all up. Beth, also,

told me about fire getting started in the closet of her bed room. The

small electric stove she was using ignited a fire after she had turned it off.

I just didn't pay a lot of attention. I thought everybody was making up

stories.

Beth, had been doing so well when she and Derek, lived in the house for the first few months. She and Rose had established such a

warm friendship that complimented their talent. They had started a small

business together. The Boutique pieces of so many different animals

and choices of images, they were making, were all, just remarkable.

I, of course was not being all that observant during my short

live in visits there. I slept in the 2nd bedroom across from Beth's room.

She came up to me one day and, said, she had heard foot steps on the

stairs at night. I didn't think much about it. It was only years later that,

both Beth and Jacob, told me about their encounters.

It was after they had moved out, that Beth came clean, with the

details about the fire that got started in the closet of the bedroom. The

shocking thing about her encounter, was, that there was nothing in the

closet that was flammable. Yet, by the time she woke up,the fire had pro-

gressed into a full blown wall fire, and, she lunged at the fire, putting it out completely with her hands, without being burnt. It was, as if the *fire*,

was an apparition.

I'll have to give Beth a lot of credit, regarding the experiences

that she continued to have at that place. She surprises, even me. I don't

think I have ever met anyone, so unafraid. She seems to blend in, or

rather, tolerates the 'other side' in a casual and unaffected way. To

top things off, Beth found a resolve that would ultimately free her from

the noisy, disturbances, but, she surely found herself dug in deep. The

house had a past. What is odd though, is, that all that time I had visited

and spent so much time at the house, I never did really see, nor identify,

then, any kind of phenomenon.

Berry, Mr. Familio, was one of our closest friends in Los Luna.

He was raised by his aunt there. The three of us loved Berry. He would

become an associate that, would later, be involved in the many twists and turns of our little reunion. Beth, became very close to Berry. She in-

vited him to reside there in that house. He became instrumental in

helping to care for Jacob. He played guitar and sang well. This guy

was surely not someone that simply wrote off the idea that there was

more than one restless spirit in that house. He told me, long after the fact

that he witnessed Jacob, chasing a butterfly in his room. It was the

middle of the winter, in the dark early morning hours. That was one of

the few, pleasant experiences, Berry remembered.

I just got off the phone with Beth tonight. She went in to

more detail about the many, many noises, foot steps and confusion. After

hearing about all this stuff, I thought to myself, wow, these are all the

typical, classic accounts that, if you are paying attention to the programs

today about the other side, you would agree, that it is probably, in most

cases, not something made up. I never did know that Berry became so scared, more than once, that he just plain split. He, had to move out.

For some reason, I just wasn't affected by the occurrences back

then. I was in and out so often, that, Beth said, that she just remembers

me meeting her on the stairs asking about all the noise upstairs, and, who

was there visiting. She said there is no one here, and I thought she was

lying to cover for Derek, who didn't want me to know that he had a bunch

of visitors. I waited for them all to leave, so I could go up and go to bed.

Then later, I found, that, there was not a soul upstairs. I remember, it not

scaring me. I never suspicioned having a bunch of voices coming from a

room, and there not being anyone there. I guess, I thought at the time,

that the house was completely safe and did not have a past. I did not know

that house was haunted, until years later. My fourth encounter with a

spirit in Phoenix, also, revealed itself in a similar way, which, I will talk about in chapters ahead.

I think the experience I had in Washington, seeing the odd guy

come out of the floor, is something my mind continues to try to somehow,

erase. It's almost like my psyche is saying, "Well, you saw something that

really scared you, but, it was never really proven to be anything but a

dream or a delusion". So, I've spent my life, up until my encounters in

Phoenix, not really being affected enough to engrave any belief in stone.

To believe that people who no longer have a brain, that's alive, can think,

attack and manipulate people, places and things from another dimension,

just doesn't make any sense to me. Life after life, is so mysterious.

Tonight, I surely did not find Beth short on flashbacks, of the

many different scenarios there at the house on Santona. She also

mentioned that there was noise that she heard extremely loud while

trying to sleep. She had cast iron skillets, a lot of tin pans and metal cups.

On many occasions, she would be awakened by something that

sounded like someone taking a skillet and a pan, and, beating them to-

gether as hard as they possibly could with extreme force. She may as well

have said, "Boy, don't get me started."

It's hard to believe that all this stuff was going on during the

many trips I took, while Beth and Derek continued to live in that

ridiculous house. I stayed with them again for just a few days while

working to save some gas money to return to the fountain, in my pick-up

camper. Again, at this time, I was pretty head strong about returning to

Arizona to live with these, fantastic gurus' I just met. I parted ways

with Beth, once again, along with, Derek, sleeping with his eyes open

and, living every day, with the terror on Santona.

8

ALTOZUMA

Mostly because, I have marbles for brains, and, a curiosity that

could have shortened my life, I returned to Arizona. I was so impressed

with these people I had met on my way through Utah. They made me feel

good about myself-something I was very short on. For the first time in my

life, I felt the unconditional love. Salina, was turning me on to a uni-

versal love without an I.O.U. It was not a sexual thing at all. She

shared with me what she had gathered and attained about *values*.

From that point on, I began to patch up my self esteem. I was finally

learning the importance of values. Inevitably, I started to see some self worth.

Salina, was, a very special lady. She was raised in California. She

journeyed up to Oregon after meeting her first husband, and, they moved

for good reasons. The two had three kids, and, split up after several years

together. She married, 'Sam Sheldon', whom, I later found, to be, a very

enlightened character also. He is a Psychologist in Bothell, Oregon. He

and Salina, parted ways prior to her meeting up with, and, traveling

South with Jimi. To make a long story short, I think all of these folks just

simply needed a change.

I managed to get rides back to Los Luna, OK. I stayed a few

days, packed a few things that included a new skill saw and, I headed

back to Arizona.

Shortly after I arrived, all of the children, mothers, Jimi,

Salina, and Amber needed to go into town, Altozuma for supplies. I soon found, that, I had just traveled 1300 miles to pick up, my pick up, so, I

could be everybody's pick-up. I didn't mind so much. I was so young

and full of life, and...I found a lot of reward and excitement just being

there for, and, with those precious people.

Altozuma, is a small village about 50 miles south east of Tucson.

It was surprising that some of these characters, back then, would choose

this area to try and make a self sufficient community work. Because,

Altozuma is a cowboy town, there was unfortunately an element

there that would eventually prove to be the death, of the freedom lovers

independent commune.

The first time that I got a ride with this crew in the convoy, on

their way to Mexico, Jimi was a different guy. He smoked pot, cigarettes,

opium, took reds, dropped acid, ate & smoked Peyote and mushrooms

on a daily basis. Jimi, was fanatically involved with the 8 part book of

Carlos Castaneda. It was a trip, just to be around Jimi. A part of him

was just plain interesting. He was so preoccupied that, to describe his

demeanor, one would have to fit, genius into the picture. I believe

that period of Jimi's life taught us all many lessons.

All of us, were the kind of people, who were trying to find the 'Light.' We

were seeking *truth*. There was, and is, no such thing, if you will. We all

were discovering more each day that it was going to take, many truths

to sculpture a rock solid discovery of what is real. I feel in my heart,

very strongly, that Jimi finally found a light for his pathway, because, he

finally did quit all drugs and mind bending substances including

cigarettes and alcohol-which, in the end was the culprit, that killed the

Fountain. Last time I asked him about his, so called, home down there, he

told me the situation became impossible. Jimi, was not a drinker. He

explained to me one day, that, several of the members and a few rednecks spent all their money and, tore up two or three vehicles purchasing, case

after case of booze, all in two days. The idea of becoming self sufficient

in a commune setting, pretty much came to an end. I guess Jimi, felt like

he needed more co-operation if he was going to continue to be involved.

It wasn't long, after all that chaos, that, the Fountain deteriorated.

Years before all that mess took it's toll on the Fountain members,

I made it back in one piece with my '66 Chevy truck and Camper in 1977.

After giving several rides to the kids there, I took Jimi, Salina and

several members, 40 miles, to Nogales. We took the short route through

the very wicked mountain pass. It began to rain that day and I got to

experience the fury of the Arizona monsoon, first hand. Just after we

we returned that day, I made the mistake of leaving the truck parked

inside of the valley area. It didn't look like no river wash to me, as, I was unfamiliar with the magnitude and force of the storms down there. It

continued, that day to dump a massive amount of rain and the storm

turned out to be a full size wash. My pathetic pick-up, with my, only home

on it, began to travel down stream. It came to a halt when it was stopped

by the dam there in the river bed, and, because the truck rested at that

point, the water rose to a level around it, flooding out the engine. I had

taken off the carburetor that day when we got back. I had purchased a kit

for it, and, whoops, I guess I should have waited til the next day...

There I was that afternoon, standing on that dam, scratching

my head while Dawn, took a picture, revealing me and the flooded

vehicle looking like I needed a stupid hat on, and bubble gum on my nose.

It took a few days to find someone with a winch on a truck to

rescue my home on wheels, but, I did find a guy that offered his services.

He winched the truck on to a higher area away from the river bed, that continued to wash through, daily. I lived in the truck for a few days.

I didn't want to just walk away and leave it for junk. I had a brand new,

one and a quarter horse power skill saw, in the camper, along with a few

valued items-everything I owed, in other words.

'Rattone,' I never knew his last name, was one of the original

members that had settled there at the Fountain. He had built a rock

house just above the area where the well was. He came by to greet me,

where I had my truck parked. I made the mistake of letting him know

I was going to hitch hike out to New Mexico to get a truck to tow me out.

He happened to see my $125 dollar skill saw there in the camper. He tells

me that he will keep an eye out-that the truck will be safe, secure and, not

to worry. Before long, I was back on the road with my thumb stuck out

on my way back to Los Luna.

I don't know how, but I convinced Derek, to help me out after hitching back to New Mexico. I guess he needed some time away from

work. He was probably curious about Arizona, and the Fountain. Some-

how I talked him into using one of his company pick-ups. We drove

675 miles, back to where my truck was stuck, with a completely

flooded out engine, full of sand.

Words don't describe, the degree of intensity, of that rocky road,

from Altozuma, to the Fountain area. I'm surprised we even got down

there, much less getting back out, pulling that stupid pick-up of mine. I

still, can hardly believe that Beth, went with us. The three of us traveled

all that distance, and back, without an overnight sleep, but, we did it.

Derek used an A frame tow bar, and, we were back without problems. The

only loss was, that, sure enough, 'cave man Rattone' did break into the

camper and took the skill saw. He probably got $10 dollars for it. I didn't care. I was just glad to get back in one piece.

I found some work there in, Los Luna, in construction. I worked

on Highway repair long enough to save up enough bucks to get parts to

overhaul the '66 Chevy, six banger engine. It was my second attempt.

I had overhauled the motor of the red Ford Maverick, I talked about

briefly, while I was in Fort Hood, Texas. Fortunately, I managed to get

it all put back together. I, later asked my mechanic bud, to check the

status of the motor. He came back a couple of days later letting me know

that, he, was hearing a knock in the manifold that sounded like a lifter

that wasn't seating right. The knock went away a couple of days later. So,

I ignored the problem. I guess I just wanted to believe I didn't need to tear

down the engine again, to be sure the lifters were all seating correctly.

This turned out to have an impact on events and, the subject, would have an effect on the future owner. That story could take up a whole chapter.

Maybe you agree, that, you are enjoying this book because, like I said, I

I do cut to the chase. I have to. I've got several thousand days to touch on,

and, I'm just getting started.

The flood in Arizona was enough to put me out of commission for

a while, and discourage me from returning to the Fountain any time soon.

As you can see, I was being compelled, back then, by sheer wonder lust. I

just didn't have a business head. I wish I did. I wish I would have come up

with some ideas about how to be more a an asset there in Arizona.

I do mean to point out, that the world is a different picture now,

and, I see clearly the importance of having an aim. If I get nothing else

across to, especially you young readers, please remember one thing. The

world will always be relatively the same planet. There are a lot of

elements that remain steadfast. Now days, what you do with your time will eventually be the factor that sums up your productivity. We all know,

of course, that you reap what you sow, and you get out, what you put in.

Today though, the economy has become a different animal, and, I am

going to continue to share some dynamic information with you.

I've talked briefly in earlier chapters, about the importance of

values. The suffering I've seen and felt has been something to write about.

What is sad though, is that people, think in terms, of it being their fault.

Maybe the preacher tells them that they didn't have enough faith. Some-

times people think that they are cursed. Others listen to their so-called

friends that tell them that they are weak, and, that they do not possess

the ability to solve their dilemma. Look around you today. There are people

everywhere that can't even afford shelter and ends-meet. What happened

to these people? This is the great United States! I can tell you first hand, that when you fall to a certain level of poverty, it is extremely difficult

to get back up.

   If you were to stop and ask a homeless person, on the street, why,

what happened, and where did this start? Most of them don't even have a

clue. Some do. Some don't. A lot of people should not blame themselves.

There are a lot of gray areas surrounding the sensitivity of the subject.

Personally, I believe that, going down hill, all gets started when a child is

not taught, the importance of having priorities. If my priorities, the few

I had, were not so scattered, in my teens, I would not have drifted so far

on to the side of ignorance, and, such a bias approach. Believe it or not,

children begin to develop a prejudging way of confronting people,

places and things, by age eight. This is a very crucial time in a child's

life. There will be many obstacles and reasons that a lot of children do not operate from a solid foundation. A kid doesn't stand much of a

chance at success without practicing the idea of using priorities that

gives him a firm foot to stand on. Unfortunately, without all of these

ingredients, you can bank on a person not seeing the need to develop

a set of priorities. Not having a foundation to work from, is like flying

an airplane, and not having a runway, at an airport, to land.

All I seemed to be concerned with, was, necessity. The people I

met, that were all at the Fountain at that time, were also functioning OK,

but, they had nothing more to share, than, necessity. Why would they?

This was 1977. We were lucky to fill our stomachs once a day there, at

that commune. All of us were so much more concerned about our

geographical location and being independent of the cultural society, and,

boy, that would not compute these days.

I got the truck up and running again. I was so proud. I thought it would drive to the ends of the earth. It seemed to be fine.

It wasn't long before I got it in my head to go visit Daniel, in

Montana. It was a sixteen hundred mile trip. I was so used to making a

quick decision to relocate at the drop of the hat, that I didn't realize that

this could end up being a one way trip. I took off on that ridiculous, aim-

less journey, for no other reason except, to simply go visit Daniel. I landed

there with zero dinero, but, the engine did hold up. At least the truck

got me to Montana.

It was the first time I met Daniel's parents. Both of them were

so warm and excepting of me. Neither of them were the slightest bit con-

cerned about me eating off their table each day. I felt like a mooch, and,

I offered to weed out their garden. I did contribute to the many chores

that surrounded their ranch. I ended up asking Daniel, if he wanted my

pick-up camper. He offered me $750 bucks which, I gladly excepted. Even though I was welcomed there with that family, a light went off in my head

while tending to their garden, one day. I was reminded of the enlighten-

ment I had experienced being around Jimi, Salina and friends. I began

to miss them, and, longed to return to an environment that was not so

materialistic and commercialized.

I must have been keeping in touch with Salina. She did write

letters. We shared a lot in common, and I loved being around that party

of pioneers, whom, were all now back in Oregon. I had their address

there. I made the decision to hitch there for a visit. I had that money from

selling my home on wheels to Daniel. Jimi, welcomed me with open arms

after I let 'em know I had enough to purchase a new chain saw. That was

a welcomed asset for all of us, because it meant having the tool needed

to cut cords of firewood to sell. There were local families that were happy to buy the cords on a regular basis, while the three of us lived in

an old country house. The place had probably been there since the 50s,

but it was shelter from the storm. We were surrounded by black berries.

They grew wild all over the western part of Oregon, and, you could eat

black berries to your hearts' content where we were.

The summer, that year, was unusually dry. It began to rain that

September. We ran out of places to cut firewood with all the competition

there those days. We had worked pretty hard July and August, and, I told

Jimi, that I left my recurved bow with Daniel in Montana. I guess he, too,

needed a break, and, the two of us decided to hitch all the way back to

Montana to pick up that stupid bow and arrows, there on Daniel's ranch.

I'll never forget how puzzled he looked when Jimi, and, I physically

walked on to the ranch property. He must of thought I had gone insane.

To hitch hike from Bothell, Oregon to Colfax, Montana was not just a one

day trip. I think, those days, people like us considered such a trip to be

a spiritual journey, a learning experience. It made us both feel free, and,

good about being able to break away from the grind without a whole lot of

money. We basically took no money on that trip. The rides we got never

made us feel like bums, because, we weren't bums. Most people in the 70s

were poor, themselves. It was not unusual for people to share a snack

with hitch hikers. That exchange was very common. Drivers would love

to hear our story, poems and conversation.

I didn't feel like a financial failure those days. If a person felt un-

successful five decades ago, it was not because of a mental illness or be-

cause someone had been bullied most of their life. Guys were choosing

to drift around as a learning experience. Nomads, were considered to be enlightened 'heads'. You never heard the word, 'homeless.'

Today, there is such an emphasis on financial success, that

people are going as far as suicide. Marriages are collapsing. Spouses are

resorting to murder, for a life insurance pay off. The influence now days

dictate, that, if you are not self employed, making at least fifty grand a

year, you're getting left behind. To some degree, this, is not so far off.

If you are barely paying your bills, you *are*, struggling, you don't have

vacation time, and, you do have, to take stock, of what you spend.

It's important, now, to take a good look in the mirror and ask

yourself "where do I stand"? "What do I really want"? "Where am I really

headed"? "Do I really have an aim, goal or destination"? "Am I failing be-

cause a doctor told me I should be messed up in the head because I was a-

bused and/or bullied, and, I did not have a guru, to show me a way out?

Let me reassure you, that, if you are asking yourself these questions, and stuck, in this hum drum, you are not alone! I wish I had all the

answers, but if you are thirsting for knowledge, and are open to a way

through this jungle, you, are well on your way out. You, have kept

an open mind up to this point, and, you haven't rejected anything so far.

I surely don't want to sound like a crabby ole man who is trying

to say that the world used to be a wonderful place, and, now it's gone. I'm

not saying that at all. In fact, it is my intention, to remind you that the

world is still, and, always will be, a wonderful planet. You just can't hurt

a world that has been around for four and a half billion years, and destroy

it in the time we have been bombing it, trying to destroy each other.

Remember that, **man** has always, been crazy. We've simply found a more

sophisticated way of beating each other over the head. The Earth re-

mains. This beautiful globe is resilient. It recovers, and, it will treat you as well as you treat it. Make no mistake, we are going to be here for a long

time, so, let's make the most of it. I want to share with you the reward

and benefits of understanding, cause and effect in chapters ahead.

We paid our respects to Daniel, his mom and family, and, Jimi & I

were back on the road, headed, west to Oregon. For the remaining fall

months Jimi, Sawn and I, cut, hauled & loaded Christmas trees. 'Sawn'

was a totally cool kid. He was so young and full of creative energy. He

went with us a couple of times to cut firewood. Now, the three of us were

stuck on the tree farm in the most miserable weather you can imagine.

For 8 long hours I would lift, sometimes, three water soaked, Christmas

trees over my head, to load on to the trucks. I would already be wet, even

with a rain coat on, by the first hour after we began our day. The temper-

ture was usually in the 40s all day. I really can't remember a more miserable job. Luckily, it only lasted a month and a half.

The three of us took that job, because, we did, have an aim. We

had all decided to return to Altozuma. The Fountain was still teaming

with commune members at that time. I can't tell you how good it felt to

be done with those Christmas trees, and, leaving Oregon for the winter.

By this time Jimi, and Salina, both, needed some time to them-

selves. I was an idiot, but, I was sensitive enough to understand, people

do need their solitude. I was single. I had a tendency, in my 20s, to cling

to people, perhaps a little too close. I loved both of these Oregoneers.

They decided to pack it all in and journey back to Arizona without me.

I must say that I was offended, and felt rejected, mostly because we were

all basically in the same boat. I had been contributing to our cost to live in

that run down shabby shack. I had also built an out house for the whole family. I dug a large hole as a make shift septic tank, that, was working

real good. I was surprised that they decided to leave the whole kit-and-ka

boodle. We were all a bunch of nomads. I suppose there was nothing

wrong with wonder lust back then. It was a different exchange in that era.

It was very common for people to move from state to state. I was too

dumb to realize that the grass on the other side of the fence was not any

greener. It was just a different kind of grass.

This departing of ways, with Jimi and Salina, marked a very

significant time in my wonder years. I was writing a lot of songs. After

spending all that time with friends in Oregon, and, singing so many Dylan,

Jackson Browne, Waylon, Willie and Hank Williams' songs I got petty

creative. It was inspiring for me to branch out and travel alone for a spell.

Days, soon turned into weeks. Weeks then turned in to months, on the road by myself. I told Jimi, I would meet them in Altozuma, but, I realized

I really wasn't familiar enough with trying to make settling down per-

manent. I was too scatterbrained to be much of a benefit to them, or to

myself, at the Fountain. I got out on the road and hitch hiked from state

to state for the next two years.

    I had been keeping in touch via mail with Charles, who was now

in Texas. I was finding farmers needing help at there ranches and pro-

ductive facilities in Missouri, Texas, Oklahoma, Kentucky and Tennessee. I

would work a week, make a hundred dollars, and, hit the road again.

Staying in touch with Salina and Charles, seemed to be very important to

to me those days after living in Oregon. I really learned a lot from Jimi &

Salina. Charles, had a lot of advanced and unique knowledge that he

shared with me while living with him, the first time, in his Tipi in 1976.

After living on the road for several months, I made it back to

Northern California. I found some work on the coast. I began to miss the

folks in Altozuma. I got back out heading South. After reaching Monterey,

I got rides to the edge of town along highway one. I had my thumb stuck

for just a few minutes, when, a large old milk truck, painted blue, saw me

and pulled over. I had a guitar with me. I think the two girls that were

traveling east together, recognized me as a possible asset. I believe both

of them were hoping that I could compliment what they had set out on

the road to do. 'Francis Shue' had some equipment and garments along.

She had been performing a street comedy act. She was good, and it was

surprising how the stunt attracted folks in a such a short time when she

found a good spot to work. I don't remember much about her act, but,

looking back, I recall both of them liking me, and wishing I would stick around, and, be a part of the traveling show with my guitar. All

I know is, I became uncomfortable traveling with two women. The other

girl was a bull dike type lady, yet, she was the one that constantly

wanted sex. I just wanted to get back on the road alone. I asked them to

stop and let me off at the intersection of Speedway and the freeway in

Tucson. I will never forgive myself for going a separate way that day. I

did not see the tremendous opportunity that offered itself with them. I

know I could have been a part of that act. I was so tired, and, was also

suffering, road burn out. The day before they dropped me off, their truck

would not start that morning after we had spent the night right next to

the California coast. Back then, you could find a pull off, and, spend the

night next to the sea without a cop coming along, give a ticket fine in the

middle of the night, and, be told to move to a KOA campground. Just as fate would have it, though, that night, still haunted us.

When we woke up, the engine was just plain dead. I pulled off the

engine cover, and, found the distributor cap saturated with sea water.

The humidity, from the crashing of the waves, was so great, that it found

it's way to the motor, as sealed as it was. I took napkins, and did the best I

could to dry the points and cap. The engine eventually started. We were,

again, on our way. Those two girls surely began to see me as quite an ad-

vantage. I only wish the feelings would have been mutual.

I was too blind to see opportunity during that era of my time in

California. I ended up going back down to Altozuma to visit Jimi & friends

for a couple of weeks. I was just a couple of years late. I had told them I

was was hitching straight there, from Oregon, after our good time, on the

Christmas tree farm, in 1977. They were glad to see me, but I had no reason to stick around. I again, was too wound up for settling down at the

Fountain. Little did I know, at the time, that Altozuma would prove to be

lot more useful and significant than most of us ever imagined. I never did

like the 17 mile distance from that village to the Fountain. That rocky,

and poor excuse of a road, that snaked through the endless hills is

ridiculous. It was never really cut to form a roadway, by a catapiller

blade. What little road there was, got more washed out every year

during the monsoon. As wiped out as the pathway was, though, stars like

Jordon Seals and others found that area perfect for making movies

during the winter months. Seals, filmed an episode of 'Poor & Famous'

there around 1985, called, 'Hell on Earth'. It turned out to be

one of his best. He paid several locals to perform small parts. I am very

impressed with that particular episode. There was another movie filmed

there called 'Sid'. I thought the producer did an excellent job with that story also.

Jimi and Salina had a child together in Oregon around the time

I lived with them in the late 70s. They produced the most beautiful,

healthy and precious little girl I have ever been privileged to witness.

It was great to visit all of them, and, get to see their little girl again.

They named her Pearl, She has turned out to be

a real jewel.

Altozuma, really took it's toll on a lot of people. Young families

would come there to escape the rat race of the cities, only to find, a very

difficult survival challenge in Southern Arizona. There was a mysterious

enlightenment you felt when spending any time around the California

Fountain. I think that feeling will continue to draw people in. The small

mining town they named 'Ponder,' that, is just over the hill to the South,

will, no doubt, continue to arouse the curiosity of people riding horseback, or going on a hike. You can also get back to Altozuma to find plenty

gas and food. The, Los Amigos pub, has a unique pool room, bar & grill

there. I found myself mysteriously drawn, for some reason, to Altozuma.

9

ONLY WAY TRAIN

The book 'Bound for Glory,' found me, when I was so mobile in

1977. It was ironic to come across a story that presented itself so close

to the lifestyle I seemed to evolve into, without a lot of choice. For one

thing, I didn't know it, but I had absolutely no direction home. I was so

used to not having a place to hang my hat, that, seeking a homestead was,

just not in the cards, and, that was OK. Obviously, I was getting

my education on the road with, hands on practical application. My future

seemed to be spelled out for me. No matter what I imagined in my 20s, there seemed to be an inevitable pull on my decision making. I would

simply look at a map, and, I would hand pick my next stop over. What

else was a nomad supposed to to do? Each of us is ultimately alone, and,

in the end, most of us will make the final choice about where we

want to be. We have that choice in the United States. Unlike countries

being ruled under a dictatorship, we are pretty much left to decide what

we want to do with our lives. Our future though, can become something,

soon enough, that we can't always control. I would surely reverse my

past, but, this is the message I am trying to get across in this story. I want

to strongly encourage readers, now to take a good look at what really

means something to you. Do you feel like you are being controlled, or do

you believe you are bound for reaching a target that you have chosen? Is

your aim attainable, or are you frustrated with past decisions?

'Bound for Glory,' written by Woody Guthrie, is a real classic. It

caught my attention because, the man made a statement. He was on the

side of the working man, and people who were living on the edge. Things

were a lot tougher in his rambling days, and he wrote songs that held up

the moral for hundreds of nomads seeking jobs, and shelter from the

biggest storm of unemployment during the great depression. He lived out

the dust bowl of the dirty 30s. The man was tough as leather, and I found

quite a bit of wisdom in his stories. It helped me through some of my

most challenging years.

I had already been traveling alone, and had developed that way

of life before I even heard of Guthrie. His book surely had a lot of pull

on my perspective. I began to not worry so much about colors, and which

route to take when reaching forks in the road. It's amazing how much of an impact our parents have on us. Olla, would buy a used car or make

a transaction somewhere, then, she would come home and cry for hours

proclaiming, that, she made a wrong decision. She would be full of re-

gret for days afterwards. I can't tell you how important it is, that, making

a choice, and, running with it, without regret, needs to stop there. If it

turns out to be a bad, or, unproductive choice, it IS correct, because, you,

learned something from it! The rocky road that, we all, walk down, is full

of extremely important lessons, that are not found in a classroom. Woody

Guthrie gave me a very positive perspective on people, places and things

in America. The man walked inside of a very brilliant light.

Purpose, is a word, I have always had a problem with. When you

are young, you don't worry much about where you are going. My mother

used the word purpose a lot, but, she was talking about the so-called holy, divine, mysterious purpose of God. I heard this word, coming from her so

often that it became obnoxious. That approach would prove to be a

pretty negative influence on me. It has been, only recently, that, I have

had the luck to run across some vital information about purpose. I guess

it is better late, than never on that subject. It can be said and shared in

a single paragraph. 'Your purpose' is what you are good at, because you,

you can pull it off without a lot of effort. You do it with a passion. Your

heart is in it, and, you are instinctively able to apply it, because you

naturally and inevitably applied yourself in that area of research!

Me, I got off the boat. I ventured out into idiot territory, looking

for some free mangoes, and, almost got devoured by tigers more than

once. The vultures have consistently been waiting for me to come along

to remind me how little I know about overcoming obstacles and,

discovering my purpose. It is true. I have lived my entire life, not really taking 'Purpose' seriously. Your values, and self esteem, both play such an

important role in this application. I am suggesting, that, in this day and

age, if you are not clear about what you are best cut out for, I will

recommend some very interesting information. My whole outlook on

life began to shift after reading a book called: *'Why People Fail.'* What

is so good about this book, is, that, in the long run it is not a book about

failure. It is a book on what to watch out for, so, you can be successful.

It is written by one of the most valued business motivational speakers in

the world. His name is Siimon Reynolds. I highly recommend this

material. It is available with @ Amazon.com

During the year of 1978, I was sitting in a business office one day,

reading magazines. I came across a story about a guy, in National Geo-

graphic, that literally walked (hiked) from Minnesota to New Orleans. It was about an 1800 mile trek. It took him a couple of months. I read the

whole story. The thing, that I found to be most interesting about his

journey was, when, he ran across 'The Farm', just outside of Banner,

Kentucky. Joey Allen Jones, had also brought his dog along. I'm not

sure how he heard about the Farm. 'The Farm' is a commune that got

started in the early 70s. A Flower Child, one of the original Hippies

that hung around and protested in the JoAnn & Palm crossroads

area in San Francisco. He turned out to be a leader, if you will, and formed

a group of followers with a common goal. Frederick came up with the idea

of pooling with someone that helped him organize and coordinate a

plan to purchase land in Kentucky. They scraped up the funds to get a

convoy of buses, and, transported quite a few team players to the land

a couple of miles from Banner. He and his followers planted and

raised several acres of pot, and was successful at selling the Marijuana at first. The law found 'em out, and Fred, went to jail for a year. He

served his time, got out, and continued to be an asset, found other ways

to generate capital, and the Farm survived. Last time I heard, they

built a fire station, an urgent care center, and, a large dinning area to

accommodate the many folks that believed in the commune idea. They

managed to purchase seven hundred acres, and they were doing well

around the time I hitched through to visit. I stayed and worked in the

fields, planting vegetables for a couple of weeks. I got to talking to one of

the members that had been there a while. He said he was familiar with

the story in National Geographic. He went on about Jones's visit, and,

that his dog was killed by one of the tractors on the farm. Joey, concluded

in his write up, that, he felt very oppressed while living there. I did too.

The so called enlightened personnel there, were very bossy. The combination of, constantly being told what, and, not to do, and, loosing his

dog, Jones' had very little good to say about the farm. I, too, felt very

oppressed while trying to fit in. I guess I shared some things in common

with Joey, because I did not stick around long either. I suppose they had

been over run by too many outsiders that had been uncooperative and/or

trouble makers. It was a little bit like the dictatorship at the place in

Texas.

I got back out on the road, and, headed to North Kentucky for a

second time. I decided to make the attempt to visit Olla, who was staying

there with our Grandmother in Saint Matthews inside of Louisville. I man-

aged to get into the out skirts of town, and caught buses to complete my

journey there for one of my last visits. It wasn't long after that, that our

Grandmother Lupe took a spill, and ended up with hardening of the arteries. That was pretty much the beginning of the end for our granny.

I stayed there for as long as I could. I got so aggravated with Olla,

after a few days, of her pushing the Jesus thing down on me, that, I ended

up having to split the scene abruptly, and attempting to hitch back out

of Kentucky. An interesting thing happened that day. I had asked Olla

to give me a ride to the edge of town. She dropped me off, but, I soon

became very distraught and undecided. I was growing tired, by this time,

of my hitch hiking days. I was beginning to crave having more security

and, stability. Hell, I didn't care much about having a home. I just needed

a good job that offered something more than a low wage with incentive

to give someone a reason to want to settle down.

I got off the road that day. I walked to a pay phone, and called my

my mother, Olla. This was one of the few times that I actually asked her for some help, admitting that, maybe, I still wanted to sound grateful.

Bless her heart. As she grew older, my poor mother sure wanted to call a

truce. She just didn't know how to make her love for us, work. I think

that she was beginning to be a little more practical at that time. She must

have begun to see that she was repelling Beth and me. After years of

driving a wedge between us with the fundamental Pentecostal over kill

approach, we were ready to just plain check out and wave goodbye.

    She got back into her car, and drove back to where I was to pick

me up. We came back to Lupe's place. I hung around a while. It also

dawned on me, at the time, that, after spending half of my life with warts

all over my hands, that, I was fortunate enough to have a family member

with a magical ability. All my warts were gone. From that time on, I have not had a single wart. I also did the best I could to get along with Olla. I

stayed a few days in Louisville with her, and, Grandmother, not

realizing, it would be the last time I would see our grandmother alive.

I can't remember how I finally made my departure from Saint

Matthews at that time. I think we went back to Texas, but it wasn't long

before I was back out out the road on my aimless plight.

Growing more, curious about what happened to Troy's boys

ranch, in Oklahoma, I decided to hitch through there during that summer.

Olla, was living in Texas at the time, and she was just South

of that area. I finally got rides all the way, into, down town South Fork. I

came to a barber shop on the main drag. I went in inside to find a couple

of old timers that looked like they had been around a while. When I

mentioned 'Lake Side Boys Ranch' Their heads perked up. Those two

guys knew all about what happened. The one man said, the place was shut down. The other guy said that, Troy, had gone to jail. They went on to

explain that, the law came in with evidence to convict Troy. I, finally got

to hear the truth about Troy Jonathan. The men, then, went on to say

they found him guilty of child molestation, and Troy was serving time. I

was surprised, and disappointed. I really wanted to visit the ranch, but

it took all this time and factual events for me to finally believe that Rizzio

and the other boys were not kidding. They did not like Troy, those days,

when we were all at the ranch, and, I really thought they were making

up stories. The two old men, went on to say, that, the ranch had been sold

at an auction. I thought to myself, not having a car, that, it would be

pointless to attempt to get out there, and, be stopped at the gate by new

land owners. I wanted, so bad, to go back there for a visit. It had been over

ten years. Those two lakes there were so full of life. That whole terrain was teaming with excitement, and things to do. I came alive at that place.

We did everything there. I discovered my identity & learned to drive. I got

my first guitar, and, learned to play it at that place. I learned to ride a

motorcycle, and, ride horses there. I saw my Father, there one, of the only

three times, at 'Lake Side'. I was broken to hear the news, that the boys

ranch was gone. I felt like a piece of me had been lost. I had no choice, but

to value, and, learn from all those bitter/sweet memories.

Time slips away. It has been 50 years since I was at the ranch.

I have looked, and looked for the two lakes and the two Victorian houses,

using Google maps, to no avail. It appears that new land owners filled in

the lakes, and overhauled the entire area. I could not find either house,

nor, the little brown church Troy, had there on the property. I should be

thankful to live now in an era where we have access to GPS and satalite probe capability. I still wonder about that place. Some memories really

stay with you. The events that took place, in the short time, that I was

in both boys ranches, was just down right astounding, yet, shocking and

unforgettable.

After leaving the South Fork, Oklahoma area, I headed back West.

I must say, I had met the most interesting, talented and open minded

people in California. Every time I lived there in the past, I remember

being able to find work everywhere I went. People were more than glad

to offer housing, for a person, when you proved to be working at a job. I

smoked pot those days. Very few companies would insist on a urinalisis

test, like today. It is no wonder so many people can't get and hold a good

paying job these days. A person can't even take a pain pill without

proving they have a prescription for it. Employers today, are hiring only people that are considered to be the most experienced with next to per-

fect hygiene, and, a stable work history. That, is a lot to ask, when people

can't even afford an apartment, unless, they have one, to four, or, five

roommates. You tell me how homeless people are going to deal with their

personal hygiene when they don't even have a sink to wash up at. It's OK

though. We need plenty more 'Soylent Green' to go around.

Once again, I remembered the many jobs all over California.

I got good rides back all the way to Barstow. There are four roads that

intersect there. Every time I went that way coming in from the West on

Interstate 40, I would find ten to twenty other nomads trying to get a ride

back east. The cops sat watching to enforce the rule that we could not get

on the freeway to hitch hike. We had to be on the on-ramp. This made it

very difficult to get a ride, especially when that many guys were all trying to get out, at the same on-ramp.

A man, with a good heart, finally came by and stopped, after most

of us finally went to sleep, sitting up. Six of us piled in the back of his

long bed pick-up. He said he was going to Kingman, which is exactly

where I just came from. We were all dizzy, and, turned around anyway, so

we all jumped at the opportunity to get out of that hell hole. I had

been stuck there for 2 days, and, a half of a night. We got to Kingman by

dawn. We walked for miles the next morning, and bathed in the Colorado

river that wasn't too far from the road we were on. After drinking the

water straight out of the river, we heard a train whistle in the distance to

the North. Five of us glory seekers were dreaming about getting a ride

back west without any obstacles that morning. The guy that picked us up

in Barstow had to go to work and dropped us off not too far from both the river and the train track. We felt fortunate to be so close to a possible ride

into California, or even a ride going East. It was so hot, I didn't care which

way, we all just wanted out of the blistering Arizona heat. I think it was

July when I was going through the area that year.

I don't think any of us had ever hopped a freight train in our

travels. Five of us, kept hearing a train whistle in the distance on the

horizon. All of us agreed that we ought to attempt to wait for one to come

by and get a ride out. We had, had so much trouble getting rides in the

past few days, and, I, personally, was ready to try anything that would

potentially get us out of the area. After walking a couple of miles to the

tracks, and, waiting half of the day, a train finally came along. One of the

guys with us, had a large back pack. He had everything you could imagine

in that over sized rack. Another guy was also carrying a lot in a back pack.

The train slowed down at first, being in the city limits, but, it soon began

to speed back up. What happened next was something I will never, ever

forget. It remains in my memory, like it happened yesterday. The one guy

with all that stuff, decided to, (never mind about how fast the train was

going), and, went ahead, and, threw his back pack on a flat bed rail car.

He was successful at managing to get the pack to stay on the car. Now,

the other guy threw his, over sized, everything-he-owned, back pack at

an opened box car, missing the door, and, his pack exploded into pieces.

I realized, that, in the little time we had left, that, we, were not,

going to get on the train! Just in those few seconds, the train sped up to

an unbelievable speed. I said to the first guy that got his stuff successfully

on, "do you realize, that all of your stuff, is now going 70 miles per hour,

down the track, without you on the train"? He looks at me with disbelief, and, could not speak. I, too, was frozen. All of us were spellbound.

We did wait quite a while for another train to come along. Finally

the freight was moving slow enough, and this time we all got on. The

other four guys jumped up first on to a car carrying new vehicles, and, got

into the back of a new pick-up. Meanwhile, me, the guy who thought he

was so smart, hopped on, but, remained on a empty flat car. The other

guys were yelling at me to lay down, or, stay down. Lo, and, behold their

warnings were seconds too late. The train sped up to a very fast speed,

but, before long, it was already slowing way down. I did notice

a guy in a pick-up, following on the 2 way road, along side the track. He

kept looking at me. Before long, I realized he was using a radio. The train

stopped completely. The guy in the truck turned out to be a sheriff, and,

he is now getting out of his vehicle, and running across the field in our direction. He had radioed in to the engineer, driving the train, to stop

altogether. That guy acted like we just committed the crime of the

century. It was a good thing he did not have a couple of deputies, with

sticks along, to beat our heads in like they did during the great

depression. I basically took the blame, 'cause I was on the flat bed where I

was easily seen. Before we knew it, the cop demanded we get off. He

said he could have given us ninety days in jail. I guess we must have

felt lucky, but now, we were 10 miles from the closest place to get on to

an on-ramp to hitch hike back into Arizona. I don't remember the

details, but our good buddy that lost his entire back pack must have been

laughing at the rest of us by this time. We all had to walk the 10 miles

and he, had no weight to carry.

This was one of three times I got stuck at the same place in

Barstow, California. This was the story about the first time I got stranded there. I was only seventeen. That is why none of us went to jail. We were

all under age. In some ways we would have been better off going to jail.

We all damn near had a heat stroke that day, as we had to walk, back to

Barstow. The other two times I was there, it took a couple of days to

finally get a ride out. It felt like the Twilight Zone.

There were several reasons I had become a drifting nomad. I

seemed to be gravitating into seeking the meaning of life. Settling down

and working night and day at a low wage job and/or working myself to

the bone to get through college, just didn't make any sense to me. I just

kept exploring, for the sake of thinking I could find a place that, perhaps

meant something. People who were trying to live with*out* the exchange

of the legal tender was appealing, but everywhere I did visit seemed

to have an oppressive approach on people. There was always one, or, several members, that took on a domineering dictatorship. They all fit in

a bunch of strict rules, expecting every one to give up their status as

an individual. I found that this is the primary reason communes in the

70s just didn't last. I believe that, because, I did travel to these unusual

and, withdrawn communities, I bled out that depth of my ridiculous

insatiable curiosity to discover that I related well to Jackson Browne's

conclusion. He was singing songs, back then, about finding *money*, to be

the only thing that is going to work, back then and even more, now days.

This was really an important fork in the road for me. Everywhere

I went, I found making money to be quite a challenge. Most importantly,

though, as I look back, I realize now that it was all because I was too much

of a scattered ding bat. I just didn't take an interest in a subject. I did not

apply myself with what I did best, mostly because I, did not see the need to capitalize. My brain must have had a leak.

When I lived with Charles in his tipi back at the Fountain, I

got to liking his philosophy. He was a likable guy during the first few

weeks that I first met him and the others from Oregon. I figured I had met

a friend that was a keeper. All the members of the convoy, that, I met in

1977 in Utah loved to hear me play guitar and sing, especially Charles. He

broke up with Bana. The two had developed some differences, and

split up shortly after arriving at the Fountain. I figured it was mostly the

situation that got weird and they both left Arizona.

Not long after getting stuck at the crossroads in Barstow again, I

decided to go to visit Charles in Fort Worth, Texas. I finally got back in the

saddle of my hitch hiking career. I was able to put the Barstow and train

hopping charade, behind me. I managed to get to Texas without additional

delays. Charles, and his new girlfriend, also welcomed me with open arms. I was a welcomed surprise in more ways than one. In addition to

my guitar and singing entertainment, they needed someone to watch

their rented house, there in Fort Worth, for a month. Marie, was studying

to be a doctor. She was doing quite well. I thought it was so outragous,

that she would smoke pot and, be able to study intensely, comprehending

better than she normally did, with a clear head. I thought this to be very

unusual, and, unbelievable. I could barely comprehend someone talking

to me, when I smoked pot, much less trying to remember what I would

try to read. I should not be surprised, though finding out several

years later, that I have always had an attention deficit disorder. I have

been told that, moving around so much has, probably been the biggest

contributor to my listening problems. On the other hand, I learned and

memorized over 150 songs excluding the 25 songs I have recorded with my domestic 16 track recorder. Needless to say, we can be horrible at

one subject, and simply flourish and capitalize in other areas of research,

depending, ultimately, on how much we apply ourselves. I got loving art

and music. Knowing what you love and want to do, really helps to

put you in the saddle. I was in the saddle hitching every where, mostly

because that lifestyle was an acceptable way of travel back then.

I got a job at the local car wash while visiting Charles and Marie.

They finally left. She had go to some sort of medical training, out of state.

I worked at the car wash and lived in their house for a few weeks. I found

an album by Kris Kristofferson and Rita Coolige there in the house,

and, I learned 3 of the best songs on that record. I was proud, and, had

fun singing those tunes when they got back.

Not long after Charles & Marie returned, a young guy named

Harry Forman. dropped in for a visit. He had been living in Denton, Texas, and I had met his sister, a few weeks before, there in Fort Worth.

Harry is a very down to Earth and free willed kind of a guy. He invited me,

to be a third roommate back in Asphalt, around 60 miles north east. He

seemed sincere, so I took him up on his offer. I was glad I did. I had begun

to tire of the rocky, whacky road life, and, settling down in a town full

of beautiful women sounded real nice. Asphalt still has two colleges there.

The one college is for women only, and Texas State University is highly

populated with students from all over. I really got to liking Asphalt, as

small of town that it was. I really got to liking Harry Forman.

A month later, Harry's neighbors' house burned down to the

ground, leaving 3 guys with no place to go. The three of them ended up

moving in on the three of us that night. It turned out to be a problem

that wasn't going to be easily solved anytime soon. I ended up getting real serious about finding a permanent job. I combed the streets, and

found an animal feed co-op supply needing a dairy feed truck delivery

driver. I learned the routes, and fed horses, pigs, cattle and dairy farm

milk cattle. I enjoyed the job, but, it was very low paid. If I had all that

life style to live again, I would have got my commercial drivers license

and advanced into driving a tractor trailer for J.B. Hunt or Yellow Freight.

Hind sight is so bright.

There was a lot of fun and activities going on in Asphalt. I dated

a few women, but few were interested in marriage. Telling the girls, there

back then, that, I wanted to fall in love and raise a family was, to my

regret, the perfect formula for them wanting to have sex. Believe it or

not, I was growing tired of ending up in bed with girl, after girl that, I was

running into during my drifting travels. Free love was everywhere, especially in the southwest. I have also seen programs, about life in the

70s. People being interviewed, would agree that, when you would go

out to a popular night club, or, just a simple pub, you would lock eyes

with someone. Saying "hi," became, a signal, that you were available.

You, then, would inevitably end up in bed with that person that night.

This was not an easy time for me. I was now, faced, with another

fork in the road. It was black or white. Either get on the train, or, stay off.

I had made so many bad choices up to that point, that, I had begun to de-

velop a phobia of, being really scared, and, being so hard on myself if the

decision turned out to be, not so lucrative. Like I said earlier in this

chapter, a person has got to accept the pathway they picked, and, run

with it, and learn from mistakes. I chose to get a regular job, and I found me a small studio apartment for $65 bucks a month. I eventually found

another old pick up. I, now, was going through a transformation from a

long lived 'traveling troubadour', a lot like Woody Guthrie, to some

one who is now seeing a need to settle down. It had been 10 years since I

worked, steady, and, paid rent.

I was meeting friendly girls a lot in Asphalt. I found one girl who

just wanted to screw, while I wanted to make her a keeper. Ironically, she

introduced me to a young spiritual and, talented guy who lived out side of

town. He dropped by one day while I was working at the Asphalt Dairy Co-

op. Ted, was extremely good looking, and, had a lot of potential. We

really hit it off, mainly because he was a good drummer. He had a set of

of Ludwig drums. He gave me directions to where he lived in the country

east of Coal, Texas. He, and I, would end up becoming close friends and drank and smoked a lot of pot together. I went out to visit him real often,

taking my cheap little power amp, and, guitar. We had the time of our

lives, sometimes, jamming Dylan songs, along with a large variety of

country, blues, jazz and rock songs. I kept trying to get him interested in

forming an official band. He was one of the few people I ever really got

serious with, in that capacity. I was so disappointed to find, that this guy,

Ted Nova, was becoming a serious alcoholic. He would work hard

all day at carpentry, and, drink with the boys until he was at risk to drive

home. He would drive home, anyway, passing out, soon as he arrived. He

married a girl named, Sal. They had child, after child together un-

planned, with, no honeymoon. Ted, was soon to become very unreliable.

I just didn't have enough incentive to offer him. He would have

probably gone down the tubes, even if, I had more to offer in the ways of pulling resources to organize a band. We did, do, some home recordings

anyway. We had a lot fun. I heard later, he was in a auto accident.

Settling down for very long, just wasn't in the cards for me. I had

another guy interested in playing bass. He was gay. That seemed to be

a discouraging factor, on my part, at that time. He was such a nice guy. He

was also homeless. I felt like everybody I tried to team up with, those days

in Asphalt, all had some kind of hang-up that made me feel like I was the

one with little to offer! Was I missing something? I guess I lacked all of

the above; all the ingredients. After the lack of patience, perseverance,

ambition, drive, set of priorities, and, focus, you name it, I seemed to be

coming up short of what it took to get people to want to head into a lu-

crative direction. I needed help, but didn't know how to ask, nor, did I see

the absolute need to get a team, to want, to be on my side with a common goal. In reality, I am finding it all falls into place when the subject is clear.

Clarity, seems to be the ammunition we all need to get past the starting

gun. Like I mentioned in Chapter 3, I missed the first train. By the time

the second one finally rolled along, it was just going too fast. Statements

I make in this book are nothing more than suggestions. Statements like:

"Don't miss the first train. Once you get on, don't jump off, no matter

what the cost." The mighty train can only run one way.

I met a couple of girls on my way to work at the co-op. I had been

using a bike to get there shortly after I got the studio apartment. They

introduced me to wonderful little gal named Pam Oliva. I ended up

in a long term affair with her. After working about a year for the dairy

merchant delivering cattle feed, I invited Pam and Harry Forman to join

me on a camping trip to visit Jimi and Salina at the Fountain. I had replaced the engine on the black 1966 ford I bought for three hundred and

fifty bucks. The truck held up, but, it was a tough journey. Harry didn't

even bring a tent. He was single. Pam and I, made noises at night in our

tent. I think he was disappointed, thinking we were going to include him.

It was crazy, long and awkward trip. Think about, how far we drove to

that ridiculous location in Arizona. Asphalt, Texas, just to the Arizona

border, is over 700 miles. It turned out to be approximately a nineteen

hundred mile trip. I can only speculate how the three of us held up.

We were so young, and it meant everything to us, to see such an

awesome place. There has been a boys ranch built there since I was there

in 1993. You could say that I am not the only person that discovered

something magical about the Altozuma area.

It was great to get back to Asphalt in one piece. I later got a job in a shoe repair shop just up the street from the area I originally got a place

to rent. I found out soon enough, that, shoe repair is a great trade to get

into, if you have investment capital, and, can buy your own shop.

I kept in touch with Pam. We dated a while, and, decided to move

to Albuquerque. There were plenty jobs. I promised Pam, I could do better

there financially. We rented a place, and, I soon found a job with a soil

consultation company. I agreed to swamp for a driller who was named

Jeff Roles. We were out of town for a week at a time every week. Pam,

must have just about gone stir-crazy. I Loved the job, and, it paid the bills.

After, a few weeks, we thought it would be exciting to marry. Big mis-

take. Earlier, we found some people that had lived on the farm in Ken-

tucky. We discovered, after I invited one of the members to be my best

man at our wedding, that, he was not only a non leather wearing follower, but, he was the biggest hypocrite both of us had ever dealt with. He found

everything wrong with us and claimed to be some kind of prophet. We

discovered after his wife left him, and, throwing the God thing in every-

bodies face, that, he, had a mental illness. I had seen this type of crazy

behavior in people before in communes. Fortunately, I knew how to spot

it up front, and, I knew to bow out politely and leave before it became a

volatile situation.

The word hippie is actually in the Webster dictionary. He defines

it as a person who is a nonconformist that is seeking a refuge apart from

the establishment and starts out using mind bending drugs. I saw these

places to be the perfect escape for people who were either bums or

religious zealots. I'll tell you one thing, with my background, it only took

me seconds to identify these outcasts. Some, *were* sincere and genuine.

This was the unique difference about the Fountain, Arizona. Most

of the people that ended up there were actually honest about why they

chose to be there. The honesty was like a breath of fresh air. It was a time

like no other. The revolution era of the 70s was extremely unique in every

way. There will never be another a decade like the 70s!

Pam, and I began to have differences not too long after we got

married. I, for one, was not appreciating Pam for what she was. I began to

realize that I got married just for the sake of legal acceptance. She was

uncomfortable in New Mexico, and, I don't think I was living up to her

expectations. We lived in Albuquerque for just over 6 months, and de-

cided to move back to Asphalt. We then, went our separate ways. Our

personalities seem to have become a clash. I found out later that our

astrological signs were not at all compatible. I put Pam through some trying times. Neither of us were working college educated jobs, and

money was an unfortunate issue. I got a job, and, I answered an ad for a

room that was for rent. The house sat at a busy intersection. It was an old

wooden Victorian one story. I took the room and met some very nice and

fun young people there. I had found a job at the Asphalt State School a few

days earlier, which was a couple miles south on the way to Dallas. I took a

six week course there, and, got a certified to care for mildly to severely

ill residents with special needs. It was a tough job. In fact, it turned out to

be one of the most challenging jobs I had ever tried. All we did all day was

change sheets, wash them, then give baths and showers to the residents.

I could have moved up in rank there pretty easily. It was like the army,

you could get a management position without having to go back to school.

It wasn't a bad job. If I had it to do again, I would have possibly made a

career out of it, and, retired there.

Both Pam and me, were back in Asphalt and living separate. She

initiated a divorce, and I went along with her choice. Sadly, we were

married in 1980, and, divorced in 1981.

A lot of people get married sometimes, for no other reason, other

than, because they think they are supposed to. I admire Tammy Ford and

Ben sole. They have been together for over 25 years and have never

involved the law in their relationship, breaking some records, in that res-

pect. I think they, for one, know that love is not something that can be

engraved in stone by sheer spoken promises. There is usually a lot of

money to be made in marriage ceremonies. The same goes with having

children. Yet so many are engaging in such commitments because of peer pressure with influence of the church, then, turn right around and get a

divorce without blinking an eye, but, it's all good, right? The judge made

money. Lawyers and the court made money, but, the wonderful loving

couple that quoted a bunch vows and promises, found out, that they,

didn't even know each other.

I didn't fit in with the roommates there in the old house where

I rented the room. I went to visit my cousin in Dallas one day after visiting

Olla. She was now living in Plainview, Texas. My cousin, Joe Howl, was

living in Dallas in the early 80s. He was doing some free lance

work with glass mirror doors. I made the mistake of leaving the job at the

Asphalt, state school to work for Joe repairing and installing the

mirrored doors. I worked with him quite a while. We went out of town a-

lot. It wasn't a bad job, but it surely didn't beat the benefits of the state

school. It turned out to be one more to ad to the list of opportunities that

I proved to by-pass. My lack of values, I must say, was no doubt, the

primary reason I kept passing up jobs that offered more stability. These

are priorities that children are just not born with. We have to teach our

children better than that.

I always got the blame. Family and new acquaintances would

always be critical of my decisions, but by the time I was in my 20s, making

up my mind to act I'm not so sure. I couldn't tell you for sure that if some-

one did take me under their wing, that, I would have listened. Beth, and I

inevitably, had already become so accustomed to making our own

decisions for so long, that, it's no wonder we couldn't stay put. It's not at

all surprising that we would fail to take advantage of a good opportunity

and / or land a career when it presented itself.

I guess by now you are beginning to see how much I am

emphasizing the difference between growing up in the 60s, 70s and 80s

and now. I just can't say enough about the extreme contrast.

I remained working for my cousin long enough to save up enough

money to get a mantra with Transcendental Meditation. I went to classes

in Dallas for seven days. On the last day, the Guru had me bring fruit and

a handkerchief along with me to receive the mantra. He had me sit down

in his office. I had no idea why I was bringing the fruit and cloth along. He

began to recite some chanting proverbs and slowly broke into the

specific sound of the mantra, having me hear it and repeat it.

The first thing that happened was, that, I broke into tears. I had

little control. I finally looked up at him and asked "what is going on"? He

said, that, I was letting out stress that I had built up, and, was unaware of

just how much baggage I had been carrying around with me up to that

point. It is still, routine, for candidates to continue to bring the handcer-

chief and fruit along. The fruit is for the Guru. He is spending a lot of energy, and thought process, to deliver the manta, and his mouth

becomes dry.

Ever since that day, I have found it difficult to hold back tears for

many different reasons. I changed that day. I began to see things in a

different light. It has been a lot easier now, for me to put myself in the

shoes of others, and not be so critical. It was a beginning. I wish I did not

continue to drink alcohol. I was in my 20s when I purchased the mantra. I

was a heavy drinker back then, and I believe that I could have become a

much more compassionate, dedicated, focused, enlightened and creative

entrepreneur, if I wasn't such a drinker. I also smoked pot habitually.

Wine with meals, is actually healthy, but I drank in excess, sometimes a 12

pack by myself, or, a whole bottle of Harveys Bristol Sherry Cream. I con-

tinued to drink for years, probably because, I was already an alcoholic by age fifteen. I blame it on habit, and, no direction home with horrible

influence from people I grew up around. It was hard for me to be com-

fortable around people who drank without drinking myself. Let's face

it though, if it didn't feel good, we all, probably wouldn't do it.

I began to find it a real challenge to continue working for my

cousin in Dallas. He was almost twice my age, and we were not a lot

alike. His business was looking, very hit and miss. The consistency just

wasn't there. This was not good for me. Above all else, how else can I say

it? I needed a sure and a concrete aim.

I found one of the cutest, private, reasonable, quite at first,

desirable one bed room ground level duplex rentals in Asphalt, while

working for my cousin. I had been driving that stupid 1963 Ford step

side pick-up, to, and, from Asphalt to Dallas, every day, to work in

that heat and humidity for five dollars an hour. I can't tell you with words how awesome it was to land such a sweet rental for $120 dollars a month.

When I first looked at the place, and gave the woman the deposit, and, the

first months' rent money, I did not notice the flea infestation in the yard.

The day I moved in, fleas were everywhere, and, they kept crawling up my

ankles. I went that day to get some flea poison, but did not have the time

to sprinkle it thoroughly around the yard. It had already become dark and

I hit the sack early. The fleas had not managed to get into the house, but

they would have eventually. That night it rained so damn hard I thought

the water was going to flood the house. Lo and behold, I went out the next

day, and, the rain completely drowned every single solitary flea for miles

around. There was absolutely not a single flea alive in that yard. I thought

to myself, that, this is an example of nature balancing itself, and solving an infestation naturally. How many times does this occur? Probably not

very often. Farmers usually have to push that kind of crop interchange

along to kick start insect trade off solutions so they don't have to use

harmful chemicals. I got so lucky. This apartment had a nice fenced in

yard, a covered car port, an air conditioner and a nice bedroom-furnished

with a bed and nice couch. Today, that same place, or, the like, probably

rents for eleven or twelve hundred bucks.

Ted, came over one day with his set of drums, asking me if he

could store them at my place for a few days. His life had been unstable,

and he did not have a secure establishment he felt comfortable with at

the time. I was fine with it, and I eventually set the drums up, and

jammed to the big stereo that I had set up there. He came back a few days

later, shocked with awe, finding a perfect environment I had set up to play songs,loud, without disturbing the neighborhood. I thought, for

sure I could get Ted interested in forming a serious, productive band.

We had several songs worked out, and the two of us were getting quite

good. There was even a couple of other guys jamming with us. Like I said,

in earlier chapters, I seemed to be the only guy that wanted to do some-

thing serious with the musical talent. It is a college town, and I got the

feeling that everybody I was dealing with believed that finishing school

was going to be the only lucrative project that was going to work for

them. In some ways they were right, but, if the Beatles, the Stones, Eric

Clapton, and, Led Zeppelin all believed that, I wonder, how far they would

have progressed.

Just before I moved out of the one-room rental, I met a girl

named Wendy. I adored this girl, but, she was taken. Still, I became very good friends with her. She, was so much, like the folks I met in Arizona.

Wendy heard about a smart guy, and, his seminars. She turned me on to

the idea of going through the 'fire walk' experience. I had absolutely, no

idea, of what in the world, she was talking about. Anyhow, I was game.

When she described what it was all about, me being the risk taker, with

the insatiable curiosity, I surely wanted to go through with this guy

was conducting there in Fort Worth. She warned me that it was going to

cost several bucks. I figured it was a little high, but I managed to pull the

money together, and, I drove her to the spot where it was taking place.

We noticed the men unloading railroad track size logs of wood that, they

piled up and sparked up a large log fire out back of the building. We paid

the admission at the door. Tony had a large PA system with big speakers set up at the entrance. One of Michael Jackson's songs was being played.

We sat down in the large room there, and before long this man

comes running down the isle full of energy. He looked like a giant. He

must be six foot six tall-big guy! He psyched us up for 4 hours. By the time

we were ushered out back where the fire was, now hot coals, raked into a

20 foot long pathway, we were all looking forward to walking on the Fire!

He then got out there, rolled his sleeves up, and, coached the first person

across the fire. She gets to the other side and looks down at her feet. I just

seemed to know that she made it without burning her feet. The rest of us

all commenced to do the same thing with no one having any kind of pain,

accidents, third, second, nor first degree burns. He had us all so excited,

enthused, and interested in the whole deal, that, we all came away feeling

like we just received a fantastic massage. It's hard to put it all down into words. The man is one of those people that has tapped into using a large

percentage of the mind. He describes the seminar as: "Not a class on a fire

walk, but, a message, that, if you can walk on fire, you can do anything."

Most of us left feeling pretty elated. Ever since then I have been

quite a bit more determined to finish projects I start, but, I will admit,

that I have chosen to be a victim of poverty. Sisters and brothers, don't

underestimate yourself. You have the power. You have the strength. It is

all about choice, and the limitations you put on yourself.

With the combination of continuing to drink alcohol and my

ridiculous influence during my so called growing up, I kept missing the

train. I've spent my whole life recognizing my lucky breaks, that I, did not

identify.

I drove Wendy back to Asphalt, full of positive energy and

with a new perspective on life. It lasted for weeks, but in the 70s, if you did not see a need to make better money, you would have continued to

look at opportunity through blind eyes. I don't want to be totally down

on myself. I feel now, like I wish, that I would have gone to the fire walk

experience closer to present day.

    Being, and continuing to be the small thinker that I was, I decided

to build a camper on the '63 Ford there at the place with the car port. I

made a lot of noise, but I came up with a usable shell. I decided to move to

back to Albuquerque before I even put a back door on it. I found Berry

Familio there, and, stayed with him for a few days while I finished

building a door on the blue aluminum shell, of my new home.

    I met one of Berry's friends named Connie. We became best buds.

I lived with her and her three boys for as long as I could. It was a noisy

environment, and, I decided to pack up and go to visit the friends I knew

in Oregon.

Sam Sheldon, has property on a mountain about 5 miles outside of

Ace City, Oregon. Sam was Salina's first husband. They had three kids

together when living in Southern California in the late 60s. He got his

license to practice psychology, and, later decided to homestead in Oregon.

He established his practice in Portland. He also purchased a piece of land

on the top of a mountain north west of Ace City.

I found myself headed up to the area close to Sam and his

wife Zelda. I seemed to be compelled to aim for Oregon for an unknown

reason. I guess I just needed to journey aimlessly again for no other rea-

son than, because, it didn't feel right to stay in one place for very long. I

did love to meet new people, but, my whole aim seemed to be fly by night.

I would ask myself sometimes if I really believed, that I was the one doing

the driving. Because a lot of the time I would feel like I was being pulled

by an only way train.

10

NORTH WEST MAGIC

There's no place in this wide world, like the Great North West.

The people that I met and got to know, that, were either from there, or,

moved there, all magically brought out the best in me.

The weather in all of the northern states can get so sever, that,

when people break down in their cars in blizzard snow storms, and lives

are on the line, laws come into play. It is unlawful to past people up if you

see someone stranded in sub-zero weather. I believe that, a set of very

meaningful values get started, after being rescued by a stranger. Someone

that stopped and saved your life, suddenly and magically, becomes a person you are going to value from now on. In my opinion, this is a good law.

It is a great exchange, and, this is the example I want use, in this chapter,

to talk about to degree of camaraderie, love and appreciation that I felt

being around the people in Oregon, Montana and Minnesota.

It was like a rebirth when I landed in Oregon. I did go through

Falls City to visit with Sam & Zelda Sheldon. They were living in a tem-

porary make shift yurt. Sam's son, who was studying architecture, pulled

together the outside logs for the foundation to build a primary structure.

Sam had a 3 story, 6 sided yurt with a silo bin roof, in mind. It was a

great creative venture, but, there was a whole lot of unconventional work

involved. I found it to be a real challenge to imagine it all coming to-

gether to be a livable dwelling.

I camped out in my camper on Sam's property for a few days.

They had a friend living in Ace City that came up one day and introduced himself. Joseph Dire is extremely good with pottery. He has some

of the finest works of art I have ever seen. His workshop was full of some

of the best pots in Oregon, and, he was doing well selling them at the

Saturday market there in Portland. The market there was full of life. I

never saw so many homeless and dedicated street guitar players pouring

their hearts out for a few cents. Joseph kept advising me to get out there

with my guitar and sing some songs. I looked for guys to jam with, 'cause

personally, I thought that the only artists that sounded half way decent

were people who teamed up with one, to three others. I just could not en-

tertain the idea of playing my songs all alone for peanuts. Looking back, I

realize that this angle of thinking is, in the end, what separates who will

make a living in the arts, and, who decides to find other ways to get paid.

I wish I had come from a family of musicians, because by this time, I was just too acclimated to excepting a job or contracted agreement for a

set wage or specific dollar amount for a job. My self esteem had some-

thing to do with this way of thinking too. If you don't have a specific

dream in mind in the arts, you are not going to have the drive to pull off

becoming accomplished in that field. This has been my observation.

Joseph's wife, Tina, told me about a party taking place in the

Jales Creek area about 25 miles from Ace City. I went to that party, saw

the band there, and ended up jamming a Waylon Jennings song with them

that night. 'Hondoa,' was a really unique little band that was mostly girls.

Their bass player was the only guy, and, he played several instruments to

really compliment the band. I met one of the girls, and, paid her a visit

later in Jales Creek. She was also a teacher. Like me, she could not see

herself continuing to attempt to make the band work as to make much of a living, mostly because she didn't start out that way. That band did host

a great back up when I did jam with them. It felt absolutely magical to be

jamming with a gut bass and four female vocalists when I played with

them. They made me feel so good about myself. It was fun, and then some.

I picked strawberries in a field across the road from her house for

a couple of weeks. I collected enough peanuts to fill my gas tank so I could

move on. I called up Sam to ask if he could use a hand with finishing his

3 story yurt. He was glad to hear from me, and welcomed me back to

work on his house. I did have carpentry experience, and, I blended in,

there on the mountain top, where they were, a few miles north west of

Ace City. The area was beautiful. I got there around the middle of

summer. They have their dry days, but, it is usually foggy, damp or

raining. I tried hard to adjust.

These wonderful folks that took me in and put me to work were

very open minded in many respects. Sam ended up cutting away a pad

on the side of the hill closest to the road that ended a few more feet at the

top where the large yurt is. We both agreed it would be great to build a

tipi. I cleaned a bunch of old poles that were laying around, and cut down

a few young trees, big mistake. I was unaware that the family did not

want any additional trees cut. It was my first time to build a tipi. I got

pictures of the whole process with the cheap little camera I had there in

1982. I was such a kid. I feel badly now about cutting those trees. I'm not

sure if Sam ever forgave me. To top things off, I came up with just an

outer canvas, and, I did not have a liner. The tipi did not heat up like it

could have, if I would have built it correctly, with the liner, and, then having a fire in the center. Instead, I found an old wood stove to use. I also

built an additional room in to the side where I put the stove. Come winter

and it not only leaked rain, but, the tipi did not heat up. I tried everything

to beat the severity of the Oregon winter conditions.

By December the weather began to take its' toll on my pathetic

situation. By the Christmas holidays Sam, Zelda and family decided to

vacation to visit relatives. Not long after they left, the water froze in the

pipes I had laid from the source to the tipi. Shortly afterwards the water

was frozen all over. I did not have chains on my truck either, so, I knew

that if I went down the mountain for food and supplies, I would not have

been able to drive back up. As as easily as I got discouraged those days, I

still tried my best to continue to tough it out and stick around. When

Sam and Family returned, I decided to leave Oregon, not because the elements were next to impossible, but, because I was just so unadaptive to

remaining in one place long enough to gather moss. I was worse than a

rolling stone. I was a goof ball.

I will never live that one down. I wished I'd stayed in Oregon, at

least long enough to finish Sam's 3 story yurt. I was having to tie a rope

around my waist to get out safely on to the 45 degree angle of the silo

bin roof that I was working on. There are times when we all need to think

things through, and consider the consequences of hasty decisions. I feel,

that this was a time, I could have picked a better plan, but, who knows.

I could have got back out on that snow soaked slanting roof, fallen off and

broke my neck. My regret tank was already full. I was still learning how to

erase the word regret from my vocabulary. Luckily I was finding magical

things to continue to be a part of my journey. Maybe my awareness was seeing the magic in the luck I seemed to receive. The truck held up, and,

I always found someone that needed a hand with a temporary task.

I did pack it all in and headed down the mountain for the final

slide, roll, slide escape. I made it to the bottom in one piece, and managed

to drive the highway down toward the coast without chains. I was

pleasantly surprised. The roads were icy, but dry enough to finally get

down to sea level.

It felt great to be back on the road headed South. I loved Sam and

his lovable little family. I learned a lot from them, and, I think they may

have understood my traveling bone. Their love, wisdom and understan-

ding all added to the big picture helping me find several more pieces to

the puzzle. I will never regret, nor forget the highlights and the elegance

of that area in Oregon. The peace and quiet I got to hear on that mountain brought out the best in me. Everyone, especially Sam Sheldon, had a tre-

mendous appreciation for my musical talent. He had a tape recorder we

both attempted to use to lay down some tracks, but the machine seemed

to have a couple of defects. I was still elated. I never once felt any kind of

rejection while in the presents of the fine people I visited in that region.

Up to that point, and even to this day, I don't think I've ever felt more

elated and impressed, as I did, while spending such quality time inside of

the north west magic.

11

ROCKY ROAD EAST

Freedom was a word I hardly ever used, nor thought much

about, in my days of youth. I remember hearing a lot of songs that would

talk about people needing to be free. Lucky for me, I have, no doubt

learned the value, of knowing how to liberate one self simply by choosing

to think in those terms. Perhaps it has been mostly due to my insanely

open mind, so... 'freedom' for me, was just another word for 'lifestyle'. I

never seemed to allow myself to get emotionally caught up in a bias way

of looking at people, places and things. I've always been attracted to

books & songs that emphasize the importance of *not* becoming attached

320

to anything. Ideas that have the potential to keep me from not accompli-

shing my goals, or, living where I choose, have never worked for me.

If you were to ask me to influence your child in a way to bring out the

best in him, I would first begin with helping him to understand the power

of affirmations and rationalizations. Growing up, I kept affirming ideas

into concrete that I was no good at basketball. No thanks to the many

thugs I grew up with that kept telling me I was no good, and, if I was not

born, good at basketball, I didn't stand a chance at improving the skill.

I grew up excepting the idea, that, even if I wanted to get better at

something, I would never pull it off, because I was *not* born with that sort

of gift. Alot of people get caught up in this way of believing. I always gave

up on a dream too easy because I was taught to believe all this. Thus, that

kind of influence is the perfect formula for a person to have the tendency to drift. Knowledge is power. I kept arriving at the rational-

ization that, I could not be somewhere, and, be happy too.

I was lacking confidence and determination, as well as purpose.

After having one of the most fantastic, next to nature experiences

of my life up to this point, here I was again, flying the coop. I guess I must

have felt compelled to leave, for no other reason again, but to keep afloat.

Traveling south on the coast line was a real eye opening ex-

perience. One of my last stops turned out to be in Coos bay, Oregon. I

hugged the coastal two lane, and ran across a few fishing shops. I was

pleasantly surprised to find a merchant selling some smoked salmon

carcasses. They had been filleted, but, still had an enormous amount of

meat left, and were being sold, for an amazing $0.25 cents a piece. I got

four of them, and, later, after getting down the road a ways, I wished I had

bought more. I couldn't believe how much food, those smoked skeletons had left on them. It was a large fishing area of competing merchants.

I passed through the Red Wood forest, and, headed on South. I

had no reason to stop in any large cities in northern California. I had it in

my mind to try to get a hold of my aunt Betty, who had been living in

California, for most of her married life.

When I arrived and connected with that family member and her

husband, Willie in southern California, I was really a mess. It didn't feel

that way at the time. I figured they would be glad to see me. I enjoyed

visiting and relating to her. Willie saw me, not as a friend in need, and in

deed, but, as a bloody nuisance. I couldn't say or do anything right. The

man had spent his whole life going from a secure family, high school

and on through college. Then he got involved in some kind of position

with banks, and soared from there, into financial independence. This poor guy, never in his life, got even a small taste of street life. When I

borrowed twenty bucks from him and tried to pay him back shortly after-

wards, he threw the money on the floor. I knew right away it was time to

split. I had a beard, long hair and missing teeth. I must have looked like

something that came out of the ground before Ten Buck Two was formed.

Luckily, I had enough gas money to cross into New Mexico. My

throw out bearing went out soon after I passed the Arizona state line.

I broke down with a serious migraine headache, and, I crawled into the

camper on the side of the road. A cop stopped and saw that I was in a fix.

For once, the police did something besides give me a hard time. The man

was really a nice guy. He told me about a junk yard just over the hill. The

next day, I crippled the truck the short distance to the salvage dealer. The

owner happened to be a mechanic with a half way decent attitude. He pulled the transmission off, replaced the part and stabbed it back in, all

for $95 bucks. I had $20 dollars left. I filled my tank, and, made it all

the way back to Los Luna.

Beth had lived in Albuquerque for a few months, but, returned

to Los Luna. She fell in love with a guy, and they had a darling little girl

naming her Nova. They rented a trailer and lived in it for the winter, not

far from a lake. When I returned to New Mexico, I got to enjoy the priv-

lege of being around Nova when she was a tiny tot. She was a picturesque

child. Beth, and many others, got a whole bunch of photos of Nova. She

was, and is, an exceptionally gorgeous baby. Beth, was a photo-glamorous

baby herself. Olla must have been proud.

They, later, rented a place on the east side of los Luna. I hung

around a few weeks after finding some temporary work. Before long my

traveling bone began to pull on my aura, and I was soon back in the black ford camper on my way back to Asphalt. I missed my friends there. Texas

has a way of enchanting a person in a way, like no other state, just ask

Willie Nelson. I've spent summer nights there, that, I could swear that

heaven had just fallen down on the field of wild flowers I was beholding.

I tried working for my cousin again. I went to visit him, and, we

ended up installing the glass mirror doors in Austin. We went out of town

quite a bit, but the cousin and I, just didn't share enough in common to

capitalize on progressing in that type of sales. I decided to move on.

I applied at a warehouse in Lake Dallas. Pay-less Cashways was

real busy, and, they were desperate enough to hire me and several other

guys. Man, you talk about a wild, chaotic way to make money. We all had

more fun than we were productive. I made a lot of mistakes, but we all

ended up having the time and opportunity to correct the errors.

I found a piece of property a couple of miles away that did not

have a lock on the gate. I lived in the camper the whole time while

working at the warehouse. I think the guy that owned the land came by

one day and saw me there, but did not tell me to leave. He probably had

been in a similar circumstance in his younger days, and understood.

Someone had already dumped there anyway. Texas has quite a few un-

locked property gates. There's a lot of space in Texas, but, evidently not

enough for me. I saved money camping out. I took showers in the ware-

house. It wasn't long before I had enough to drive to San Diego. At the last

minute, Olla was invited to stay with my aunt Betty up north. The

two of us did drive all the way from Dallas to Southern California in that

stupid 1963, step side, Ford pick-up camper. The transmission I bought for

it, and, put in myself, didn't even match the rear end, making the gear ratio bad, for the differential, but, what the heck. When I was young, I just

never seemed to let myself get bothered by possible catastrophes that

could have occurred. It is surprising, the chances I took. When I was

young, especially back then, I just didn't worry. A person can tolerate a

break down a lot better when in your 20s.' Hell, you can survive anything

if you don't concern yourself with having, so called, stability and con-

venience all the time.

I had heard quite a few wonderful things about San Diego. I have

always liked California, and I had always been able to find a job there. San

Diego is an industrial city with a shipping port, so, I figured I would like

to live there. Once again, I was headed back west which, temporarily, put

an end, to my rocky road east.

12

THE STRENGTH

Physical strength, mental health and eating the right foods

was not a big concern for most nomads, partiers and kids living on the

edge during the 70s. I was so mobile, and, I really wasn't all that aware

of just how many miles, I was racking up, on my external engine. I never

heard of, or, even used dental floss until I got into basic training in the

army. Kids today are lucky, if they're paying attention. We are surroun-

ded by a wealth of information about how to be, very healthy, these days.

I already had a mouth full of cavities, by my sophomore year at Durango.

After graduating high school, it is only because I was young that I man-

aged to stay above surface, no thanks to my ridiculous upbringings.

I decided to take a massage class in a school in San Diego. It is a

great school. The 'Institute if Psycho Structural Balancing' was an eye

opening experience. Yes, I had a mantra, and, I was practicing mediation,

but, this class was more than just instructions on how to help someone

relax. The instructors taught a class in Thai Chi, and I related to all of the

class members. I felt a great camaraderie with everyone in the school.

They were all very good influence on my learning. There is a lot of giving

of ones' self in the field of massage. Some Karate trainers put their stu-

dents through a full year of Thai Chi as an important part of the class. I

attribute a large percentage of my awareness and anger control, to the

grace and peace I received, taking these classes.

I found a guy looking for a room mate on the school cork board

there on the day I arrived and signed up. The school excepted my G.I. Bill

allotment that I had not used up to that point since I was discharged from

the army in 1975. I got through the class, but I found the competition to

be overwhelming. I went ahead and got a permit to practice there in San

Diego, and, I gave quite a few massages which afforded me an opportunity

to get some experience.

The '63 Ford truck, I had, seemed to stick out like a sore thumb.

I got a ticket the very first day in San Diego. Just about every month I

continued to reside there, some cop would find another reason to give me

another ticket. The police had a protocol of quota to complete each day

there. I seemed to be a target, having a vehicle that looked like a cartoon.

People said it reminded them of something out of the Flinstones. I must have got 6 citations in the six months I was there. I got my first ticket for

leaving the truck running unattended while at a Seven Eleven. The others

were all parking tickets. You could not park in an alley, or anywhere,

even with the absence of, a no parking sign. The straw that broke the

camels' back, and, really tried my patients was really disgusting. I was

parked along side the Pacific beach one afternoon, with a girl, bothering

no one. We both were so blissed out, feeling so lucky to be alive being able

to enjoy the wonders of mother nature, counting our blessings. One of the

tenants, living in the apartment behind us saw that I had one tire outside

of the designated parking space. They called the cops. The guy sneaks up

to the window and saw that we had an open beer, and a wheel off the

curb. That man harassed us and talked to us as if we had committed the crime of the century. He gives me ticket that amounted to an $80 dollar

fine. He then, walks over to the passenger side to also give her an eighty

dollar ticket and included a long strict lecture. I had been working hard

all week trying to keep up with the cost of living. To top things off, my

good friend who was with me that day blamed it all on me. With a very

hostile approach, she kept demanding that I pay her fine also. I guess I

didn't lose a lot that day, when she told me, she only wanted to see me

again if, and when, I had the $80.

There was a cop at every block, around every corner, waiting for

someone to J-walk. I thought to myself "Is this the lifestyle and tran-

quility that I came out here to enjoy"? California was at one time a very

desired state to live in.

The guy I was working for, cleaning swimming pools, made me an offer around the time I was having so much luck with the cops. He told

me that he would give me four dollars an hour, to use my truck, to clean

his wealth of accounts in the pool business! Four dollars an hour! Boy,

let me tell what. By this time, I was simply ready to puke. I can't tell you

how alone, bogged down and discouraged I began to feel at this point.

California didn't seem to have much to offer people, who didn't

have a lot when they arrived. I believe it has probably always been

that way, and will always continue to be that way, but... this was 1985!

By this time I began to question my abilities, and, my strength.

How strong was I, really? Did I really have enough to offer the world to

be able to make my rent and stay afloat? Had I been dreaming so much &

so long, that I was brain fried? I was trying so hard to settle down, keep a

job and begin to plant seeds. I was out of ammunition, short on options, &

time was not waiting around for me. My situation began to remind me of

the dirty 30's during the dust bowl storm that drove so many people from

Texas and Oklahoma, West. They tied on everything they owned to

their beat up vehicles bound for, and hoping to find work in sunny

California. Oh, they were strong alright, probably more determined

than they were healthy. Just as fate would have it, if they did not have

a certain amount of cash in their pockets, they were told to turn around

and go back to from where they came.

Woody Guthrie got off the boat alright. He simply snuck around

before he was seen at the border. He basically walked across country, and

stole his way in. After Reading about the hardship he endured, I consi-

dered myself lucky to get into California so easily. It wasn't long, though,

before I was to find myself needing to leave the state to keep from goin' nuts!

I declined the job, using my truck to clean swimming pools in La

Jolla and southern San Diego. I was soon back on the road east headed for

New Mexico, and the trip went well except for the tread separating on

my right rear tire. I had a good spare, and, I made the journey in one

piece.

After arriving back in Los Luna, I couldn't help but wonder how

I could spend all that time and effort to get out west, then, find myself

right back in the place where I, at one time, wanted to leave so badly.

Right around the time Nova was a toddler, my sister & her hubby had just

got a good deal on a fix-er-upper house and property there in Frog valley.

I helped them with renovating the house she purchased, cheap, shortly

after I came back. I tore out the shower and installed a bathtub for her.

I also got up in her attic, and, packed the whole roof cavity with fiber-

glass insulation of which got all around my neck. It itched like hell for

several days. I tried dressing, to protect myself, to no avail, but I got the

job done.

The work came to an end. I found a couple of painting jobs that

also didn't last long, and I decided to split town. Beth, and Nova's dad,

gave me some cash for my truck. I decided to hitch hike west, but, I began

to feel differently about life on the road without a target.

The only thing that was beginning to make any sense at this point

was simple. I decided to stay planted, and look into a trade that I was

suited for. I hitched to Albuquerque, and I looked up an ole friend from

Los Luna. He took me in for a couple of weeks, but, it was clear that he

really wasn't looking for a room mate. The road life was beginning to take it's toll on my mind and body. It was never easy living like a nomad.

I ran into a girl working at a nursing home. I caught a ride with

her, got a job there myself and worked a few weeks with geriatrics. Later

I applied at the University hospital. It was called BCMC at the time. I

worked there for two years in the operating rooms as an orderly. It was a

tough job. We transported the patients from the rooms to the O.R. suites.

We would then have to clean, the operating rooms with a fine tooth comb.

I never did make enough to settle down in Albuquerque and

make the town my home. I continued to work in the medical field. I took

a few shifts with a company that gets called to replace someone who calls

in sick. It paid pretty good back before most of these registries shut down

after the crunch of 2008. I took an aid job at Saint Josephs Hospital there

working on a med/surgery unit. The job was OK, but Olla got sick, was in the hospital for a while, and returned to her apartment. She was released

and told she needed a caregiver. Both Beth and I, volunteered to help her

out. I took it too far though. I decided to pack it all in to a U-haul, and,

move back to Texas, and stay with our mother until she regained her

independence. I bought a Chevy Monza wagon in Albuquerque, and put

all kinds of work and parts into it. I paid 300 bucks for the car, and I had it

running great after restoring the stupid thing. I got into a head-on

collision with a girl on my way to see a friend in Asphalt. A poor girl lost

control and went sailing against the flow of traffic on a two lane. My car

was totaled, and, she did not have insurance. I thought I was going to

have to tolerate a total loss until I met Almira Chavez. I got another hos-

pital job, working again, as an orderly. Right after my 2nd week there, I

helped her to breath by turning her to her side when she began choking after her surgery. She later got my name and contacted me to offer

a thank you. We became friends. I dated her for a while. She happened to

be an executive of a large insurance company in Dallas. After hearing a-

bout my accident, she pulled some strings. I found out, that, if you have

good standing liability insurance, and, someone destroys your bike or

your car, and, they do not have insurance at all, you don't have to take a

total loss. Almira, managed to get my insurance company to pay for my

lost time at work and my injuries, that, were minor.

   I had been used to having my own vehicle, and, I jumped on the

opportunity to work for a friend to get another car there while I was

stuck in Dallas. I ended up painting the awnings of his home there in

Carrollton in exchange for his old 1979 Grand Prix. It looked like hell, but

it did not have that many miles on it, and, it ran good. I finally finished the job on Joey and Misty Benton's home. I found a painting job close

by, and, saved enough to get out of Texas that winter. It snowed and got

real cold the night before I tried to leave. I ended up having to postpone

my departure. I was back staying with Olla. She wanted me, so bad, to

stick around. She was so lonely. I felt bad for her after leaving her to fend

for herself again. It was such a trade off. She never really wanted us

around, but, she had her limitations, and I still think she did well. Olla

somehow knew she was incapable of being there for Beth and me. Worst

of all though, her belief system was mostly responsible for her coming up

so short on the ability to care for us, as well as, for herself. She strongly

believed that all strength and resources come from her being in the will

of God, and, a person is surely weak and incapable if choosing to go ones'

own way. No one could convince her otherwise. This brings me to the most important threshold, of what I am attempting to get across to you,

in this chapter.

The strength, the tremendous strength and power that is within

the human being. The miraculous potential and creativity that lies wait

for us to use, I am here to tell you, all begins with decision. Desire plays

a very important role, and it is entirely up to you to stick to that choice.

It is only then, that strength, will manifest itself. Whatever you need to do

to get it done and be happy, all depends, on your desire to make it

happen. If you heartfully believe that you do not have the resources,

you are not alone. This is why many people go to church. Others find it

more practical, to seek entrepreneurial opportunities that fit their aim.

Whichever road you choose, you are right on target. Make no mistake,

whatever endeavor you're pursuing, does require networking, with one or several people. The strength that is multiplied with others, is inevi-

table. Don't become withdrawn like I did. Acknowledge and confirm

your power. Keep an open mind. Keep the door open, and never under-

estimate, the strength within.

13

DELGAROSA

Words are easily said. It's easy to tell a joke. Songs and

dreams come and go, but the *truth*, haunts most people. So many of us

would rather hear a lie than to face the result of what the truth brings.

Make no mistake though, in the end, the truth usually brings the problem

to the surface so we can deal with it and make necessary changes. What

scares us, is that we fear, with good reason, that we are not going to have

cooperation. People judge hard when they really don't need to. People

cop out. We sometimes, throw in the towel too soon.

Shortly after I arrived in Albuquerque, once I escaped the harsh winter in Texas, I did get a job. The Grand Prix held up well, and I found

Berry there, glad to see me, in spite of my rambling nature. I tried driving

for Albuquerque Cab Company. I did well my first few weeks, and, I liked

the job. One night I ran across I guy that had been mugged, beaten badly

and ripped off. I tried to flag down a cop who accused me of speeding.

I drove ahead of him to get him to stop, with the intent to try to get him

to help me to help the poor guy that got rolled. The cop did not believe

that I was telling the truth. Don't be stupid and do what I did. Just go

to a pay phone or use your cell and call 911. This situation got so ridicu-

lous, that, I got discouraged and decided to up-root again. I left the taxi

company because, on top of the desperation I already felt, with a life time

of betrayal relations, I couldn't help but feel like there was poor team work in New Mexico. I had always felt too many communication break

downs, in that state, among Caucasians and Hispanics. That situation re-

minded me of way too many unproductive, compromising affairs and

racial differences I had encountered in the past. This time I felt like the

cop discredited my attempts to reach for help because I was a gringo.

There's always been a phantom voice in my head that is sugges-

ting me to stay on the road, and, to not gather moss. However you want to

say it, I was raised a nomad, and, a drifter. Like I said in chapter one, "It's

scary to think how I could have turned out." I should add, that to some

degree, I should be thankful that my childhood consisted mostly of harsh

strict discipline full of many unusual lessons.

I packed it all in again, and thought that I would try settling down

in San Diego. I remember only having $400 bucks saved for the trip. I knew, of course, from being there before, that I wasn't packing enough

dough to really be very comfortable. When I arrived in Tucson, I figured

I would at least give Jimi & Salina a call to say hello. They were glad to

hear from me, and they did invite me to pay them a visit. I headed south

that night, and, arrived there around dusk. I can't tell you with words,

how good it felt to see them, and be back in Altozuma. They had built a

workable yurt, and were doing well.

After a couple of days we all went to a party at a friends' place

that accommodated a large number of people. I had a couple of beers and

ran into Salina's kids I that I enjoyed a lot. Shortly after sharing stories I

passed by a girl who was all alone, not socializing much. I introduced my-

self,and met the most beautiful girl at the party. Her name is Marzi Lou

Hampton. We were both immediately excited about making each others acquaintance. We exchanged stories that night, & woke up to a brand new

day the next morning, together. Marzi, turned out to be one of the cutest,

intelligent, compassionate, determined, bubblely, friendly interesting and

experienced individuals I had ever met. That next day we drove out to

one of the lakes a couple of miles outside of Altozuma. We walked cheer-

fully together quite a ways, and, really enjoyed each other's company.

Marzi's husband from Kansas City had passed away a few weeks

prior to the time she and I met at Fred's party. Art Jethro had been

a Kansas City cop for years after serving time in the Air Force. Marzi

learned a lot from Art, and I was to find out soon enough, that Marzi was

a walking dictionary. She did very well in school, and she worked in the

garment industry for several years before she met Art Jethro. He fell

ill to multiple sclerosis in Kansas City, and, was told by his doctor that he would feel better in a drier climate. He and she bought a piece of land and

had a house built on it in the early 80s, a couple of miles from town.

I found work in Rose Valley, 36 miles North West of Altozuma.

Marz and I, cleaned carpets together, there, for the retired residents.

It turned out to be a tremendous learning experience that put us in the

saddle for future opportunity in that trade.

The owner of the franchise there wanted to sell the business to

us, but wanted way too much for the little equipment and accounts that

he had. He had no contracts with any of the folks he was cleaning for. His

equipment and truck all amounted to $1500 bucks, and he wanted

$100,000 for the whole tamale. We didn't think it was worth, any where

near that much. Marzi, was tired of Altozuma, I was open, and, we decided

to move on.

I found a place to rent in Tucson. We moved and lived there for a few months, but decided to move to Phoenix. Without a rock solid rea-

son to live in Phoenix, we both got stressed and became discouraged with

with the many voids we felt in the big city life. I talked Marzi into moving

back to Altozuma. I had lived such a low profile and primitive life for so

long, that, I had trouble adjusting, so, we moved back south. I just hadn't

developed the business head, that I needed back then, to take advantage

of the wealth of opportunity in Phoenix.

Our friends welcomed us back while we lived in a trailer for a

while, there not far from Altozuma. We took a trip to Kansas City to visit

Marzi's sister. It was a great trip up until on our way back through

Arkansas. The Volkswagon rabbit we were driving was a good car, but, the

poor thing made it down into a camping spot near a lake and, wouldn't

go back up. It had a front wheel drive and the wheels spinned until it began to over heat. We walked back down into the deep, pitch dark forest

and found an old abandoned house. I thought to myself, if I was writing a

horror story, this would the place to give me plenty of ideas and material.

There was no way we were going to spend the night in that damp, dark,

all wood house. The road was wet, but, I managed to find a dry spot to set

up our two man tent. The next day, all we could think to do, was to walk

up the hill side and stick out our thumb. We did get a ride into a small

Arkansas town. Believe it or not, we found a guy with a winch on his

ancient Ford tow truck. The old man must have sensed we were low on

cash. He got the car back up out of the mess we were in on the hill, and,

refused to take any compensation for the favor. The ordeal brought me

to tears.

The Rabbit continued to over heat that day. All we could do is stop every few miles and add water. I found out weeks later, after we

returned, that, a bunch of debris was blocking the radiator anti-freeze

from flowing correctly. It would have been simple to fix it, had I known

it was there. We got so lucky on that trip. It's a wonder that forest didn't

swallow us up. I limped the car all the way back, and, we made it back to

Altozuma.

Marz & I lived in a trailer court there for a while. I had an alter-

cation with the owner of the place. We had a misunderstanding, and, he

hired a guy to move our trailer off the property on to an intersection up

the road from the town. Meanwhile, we were on our way back from

Tucson that day, and the car stalled. It rolled to a stop, and, in the middle

of the summer heat, that stupid car threw a timing chain. The VW Rabbits

made that year were fitted with a rubber belt driven timing chain. I would have replaced it as a preventative measure, prior to that time. The car

having a major break down, couldn't have happened, at a worse time.

There we were without a car, and, without a way to go get our

trailer out of the mess this man put us in. Our only shelter was sitting at

the junction of Horse Ranch Rd, and West Altozuma Rd, where everyone

could see the trailer, sticking out like a sore thumb, all by itself.

We got out of the vehicle that day just outside of Tucson. I took

a look at the engine, and pretty much knew, the car was fried. There was

no fix to the engine without an overhaul. We got out and walked to the

nearest junk yard.

As fate would have it, we counted our lucky stars that day. We

happened along one of the oddest, old timer, and bone yards, I ever saw.

I mean to say,that this guy, was the kind of clown that would make you

start laughing before he would even say anything. He had this great big

Airedale yard dog, that, really wasn't mean or threatening. She seemed to

know if someone was up to theft or harm in any way. The old man

must have been in his eighties. He was constantly joking, cussing, smo-

king, and spitting. He fit right in to being a junkyard owner. Thank good-

ness he was in position to help us. The guy had a Ford van with a trailer

hitch, and he was glad to help us. We all drove down to Altozuma, and,

towed the 13 foot trailer without incident.

    After getting the trailer back into Tucson, we parked and lived in

it for several hot days. We were short on money, but we had enough

food to last 'til we could sell the car and stereo. It was hot as the Sahara

desert that summer. We had an evaporated cooler I had made earlier that

did not work so well, so we ended up hitch hiking into town. I found an

extended stay motel, and we remained there until we stepped into another hell hole. Thank goodness the junk man gave us a hundred bucks

for the trailer, and another guy bought our warn out car for around the

same amount.

I lived in Tucson for a while and attended school there in spring

earlier that year. My neighbor introduced me to a guy that called himself

Ruben Tosh. He did not tell me that he just got out of jail. I misjudged his

his character. While we were at the motel there after recovering from the

traumatic situation in Altozuma, he invites us to share the rent with him

in a small, one bedroom trailer. I got some work at a daily-labor-daily-pay

office. It was close enough to ride a bike there. Meanwhile, Marzi,

remained at the trailer with him. He begins, then, to show his true colors

to her, and started waking her up in the middle of the night. The guy

gets her to go to the bank to take out money for crack cocaine. This intrusion would continue until I was also awakened. We found that Ruben

would become threatening if either of us would not co-operate with, not

only his drug habit, but, with his violent outrages. This guy would sit

with us and others and continue to talk for, an hour sometimes, about

how he is going to hurt or kill someone if he or she blows a whistle. Lucky

for us all, I personally, am not a whistle blower, nor a trouble maker. It

came down to we were going to need to leave aburptly, or someone was

going to get hurt or die.

Ruben had been dating a strip dancer he met in a place just down

the street close to Oracle Road. She became a friend. Sydney Gallegos

had been supporting her 3 kids by herself with her husband in jail. She

found, too, that she had made a serious mistake by dating Ruben. Marzi

and I, finally saved enough to move into another motel. We ran into Syd shortly aterwards, and she asks us to stay with her in her trailer in hopes

that we could all remain vigilant and safe. She realized that she needed to

break up with this guy, we called Ruben. After staying with her a few

days, I was awakened one night by a bumping and a cracking noise

just out side the bathroom window. When I tip toed in to look out to the

west, I saw Syd's car front seat on fire. By the time I got dressed, and out

side, the car was engulfed in flames. After calling 911, and getting the fire

out, the fireman investigator did determine it to be arson. We just knew

it to be Ruben, that set the fire. He lived within walking distance. He kept

putting up his pick-up truck for as collateral to get more crack cocaine.

He could not hang on to a job, and he kept scaring everybody off. Again,

lucky for him, I have never been a whistle blower. We wouldn't have been able to prove anything, anyway. Soon as our checks came in, as I saved

some hard bucks at the labor business, we finally got the hell outta

Dodge. I can't describe with words the relief we felt at that point of our

sunny days, leaving Tucson, Arizona.

You are probably wondering why in the world I named this

chapter 'Delgarosa.' Delgarosa is the name of a street in Phoenix where

we experienced a poltergeist, or an eerie entity, in 1999, that refused to

leave. I am going to briefly breeze through some short events that led us

up to that odd time of our journey. I am also going to reveal the truth

about the high school I went to in, New Mexico, in my final chapter.

I had been in contact with my sister, during this bad dream

of a pit fall we seemed to have stumbled into. She reluctantly did invite us

to make the trip all the way to Los Luna. She had been living in a two bedroom house, 3 miles south, of that tiny city in New Mexico. Beth,

really, didn't have a clue of what we had just been through. I left out a lot

of detail about everything that we survived between the time we lost our

car and trailer and leaving Arizona. Had I told her, everything, she may

not have helped. We were more vulnerable than what we were revealing.

After the first week of camping out at Beth's place, I had a

suicide plan, seriously in place. We still had our shot gun. At that point, I

I had seen too much. I was just about finished. To say I was at the end of

my rope would only be an introduction to the grief and despair that was

just getting worse. Marzi and I were without a car. We did get jobs, but we

were relying, on Beth, too much. After taking a day at a time, and putting

off the shot gun remedy for a minute, I decided that we were imposing

on she and Nova. I found a room in a motel in Los Luna. I was sadly reminded of Duke when renting the room from Samson's place there on

the main drag, on historic route '95. Mr. Samson and his wife Olinda

were Duke's aunt and uncle.

We both got a job working together in a motel on the top of New

Land Hill, there, on the east end of Los Luna. I had a bike, and we liter-

ally rode that poor bicycle together down that steep half mile hill. Marzi

rode on the cross bar and I straddled us both on that stupid bike.

It didn't take us long to tire of the low wages, not having a car,

and living in a motel we could not even cook in. Again, we saved enough

to get us back into a city that offered more opportunity. We were

learning quickly how difficult it is to recover after, dropping down to a

seriously low level of poverty. From that time forth in my life, I have

surely had a lot more compassion and empathy for individuals who can

never bounce back up due to their mental illness and related problems.

We both kissed the ground when we moved, found a job and got

settled in Albuquerque. I got a job again with my ole' buddies with the

soil consultation business. I, again, had to go out of town every week

while Marz stayed in an apartment, we found there, close to the air force

base. Both of us never really did like Albuquerque. I set our sights for

Denver. We uprooted again, only because we were young enough to keep

moving, with no other direction or reason, except for, sheer wonderlust.

Denver is another challenging city for a poor boy to think in

terms of drifting into town with peanuts, and actually settling down. I got

a job there driving 12 miles to work in highway traffic. I worked cleaning

carpets for Chem-Dry Inc. I started out working in a two man team, and

quickly soloed—making as much as 3 to $700 bucks a day, by myself. The

guy at Chem-Dry, was paying me $5 dollars, and, 0.35 cents per hour.

Needless to say, this ole' drifter was getting pretty discouraged paying

high rent, and driving that high speed freeway to work, in that beat up

Ford, I bought in Albuquerque, for $400 bucks.

Marzi and I, had pleasant memories of living in Phoenix in 1990.

We both agreed that it would be in our best interest to move back. That

year did turn out to be one of the hottest Augusts, Phoenix had seen in

decades. We arrived just a few days after it had been over 122 degrees.

It continued to be in the triple digits all that September, while we moved

into a seemingly nice apartment during the day. I found out this first a-

partment was catering to several misfits, drug selling and gang related

teens. Three weeks after living there and driving 17 miles to Scottsdale to

clean carpets for another Chem-Dry franchise, I finally landed a job at the

VA hospital. We soon found a better, one bedroom apartment, in a better neighborhood. The two of us lived there for the next 3 years.

I got a call from my cousin, Joe Howl one afternoon in 1997,

after getting off work. He said he had been trying to get a hold of me for

a couple of days. There was no other way to let me know, that, my mother

Olla, had been killed in an automobile accident. What is ten times worst,

is, that, I was not at all saddened by the news, at least not at the time. I

was 42 years old. I still had some lessons to learn about my appreciation

for family, and, people in general. Maybe I sensed somehow, that, she did

not want me to be brokenhearted. I did know for sure, that Olla, never

did blend in with very many people places and things. She was just not, a

happy camper. I think my mother saw Christianity as a something very

magical—something that was going to bail her out of the poverty pit she

kept falling back into. She had good qualities. Bless her heart, she surely did not deserve to die alone in a t-bone accident like that. I would have

much rather seen her go out quick though, than to be laid up as a para,

or a quadriplegic for her remaining few years.

We later got an apartment, not too far from where we were.

I needed more space. We now had a few more things. I had my musical

power amp and speakers along with some carpet cleaning equipment

I had invested in. This place had 3 bedrooms with a large living room,

plus storage. We found, after we moved in, that the apartment sat directly

on a street called, Delgarosa.

We were excited. This new apartment was spacious and, had a

shared grill on a nice patio. The neighbors were friendly. We figured we

had found a great new place to live! Even the manager became a personal

friend. He also met us out at Bartlett Lake and took us for a ride in his

boat. It started out a very fun and relaxed summer.

I had purchased some NSA water filters to sell when we were in

Tucson. We still had a couple. I decided to install one under our sink. I had

plumbing experience, and with a trip to Ace hardware, I managed to get it

in correctly. The air conditioner was also inside the apartment, just above

the master bedroom closet.

We had been settled in for about 6 weeks there in #101. I got up

one night to the bathroom to find the light going on and off. I figured

I would tend to it the next day. I checked the bulb. Then I checked the

fuse box. I also checked the wiring. I am not an electrician, but I do

OK with trouble shooting. I could not find an obvious reason the lights

were flickering. A couple of days later Marz was alone in the kitchen, and

the television came on by itself. It later went off by itself, and Marzi be-

gan to become argumentative a lot more often than usual. She started treating me like I was interfering with her thoughts and daily activities.

I had never been intrusive or noisy, and she had never complained before

about anyone bothering her, especially me.

Several days went by, and the lights were flickering so often that

I began to not even pay much attention. I, later found Marzi, going

into the closet, and, taking the air-conditioner apart. The inner core

was sealed and packed with surrounding fiberglass insulation. That stuff

fell down on to her face, neck, chest, back and got in her cloths. Needless

to say, by this time I began to develop a knot in my stomach that wasn't

going away. I knew something was wrong, but oddly, I was not scared, nor

did I think that we could be harmed by an unseen force. It is hard enough

to explain the feeling I had. It's almost as if the entity had control of what

we perceived it to be. I felt so helpless. I was becoming very distraught.

Marzi started calling 911. The cops would show up, and she would tell

them, that, I was verbally abusive and hitting her. They would investigate,

find that, not at all true, then they would leave. Then Tubac was called in

to access the situation. They would show up. Marzi would tell them

that I was abusing her, they would take notes (occupy a space and pick up

a paycheck), then leave. Nobody would take an initiative. I kept telling

them, that, she needs to go into in house rehabilitation and get her medi-

cations adjusted, but obviously everyone that was called to come to our

aide, seemed to be suede. It is, as if people were subconsciously removed,

from doing what they came to do. The knot in my stomach was getting

so uncomfortable I could not even enjoy drinking beer much less eating

food. We had enjoyed drinking beer together for years.

The water filter that I had installed under the kitchen sink had been working very well for the both of us. I took pride being able to hook

it all up with the tools I had. The day that I found Marzi in there, with a

crescent wrench, completely unhooking the water filter, I said to myself,

that's it! I have had enough. I began packing our stuff. I got a bunch of

boxes and found a storage unit. I wanted out more than anything.

After getting most of our things into storage I finally got some

feed back about the root of what was probably going on. I knew one of

our, across the pool neighbors was a religious believer. It was hard sorting

things out with him, because he kept talking about there being a demon

in #101, where we were. He did finally come forth with the fact that a man

did die in the house, and, that he was not a very nice guy. I wasn't com-

pletly convinced about that scenario, but it did add up. Marzi continued

calling 911. I found out 3 months later that she had developed a heart problem, and it was causing her to have serious panic attacks. She was

so succumbed by the attack in the apartment that she did not identify

the fact that, to top things off, she had a heart problem. Chances are,

with the weight of the evil we we were facing, Marzi's immune system

could have also been affected. I do know, that I was becoming ill. By this

time I could not eat at all. I could barely drink water.

After we finally got all of our furniture and living items out, we

were using the van to sleep in while we searched for another place.

One of Marzi's so-called friends we met while we were there kept sugges-

ting that I just drop her off at a motel and split. I guess we found out

exactly who our friends were. The girl was so young, a great parent and a

mother to her two children. Not everyone is prepared to handle mental

illness and a haunting. The irony, and the pay back, was kinda stiff.

The young girl wanted our apartment. She just wanted us out, so she and

her young husband could move in. The funny thing was, that, she thought

the whole time that it was just a matter of Marzi becoming very ill. She,

had *her* arrogant opinion, about what was going on in the place we were

renting. This couple did not believe that there was a very powerful force

at work. I can only imagine the unwelcome surprise when this family

finally got our apartment. We left them a large amount of our furiture,

that included, a big couch sectional and, a nice entertainment center that

Marzi bought, and put together, herself. Who knows? Perhaps she was

the only one affected in that manner. I do know that, that spirit delighted

in using Marzi to manipulate several others, including, the cops.

I continued to take Marzi driving around town, in search of an

apartment for her. I was insistent on doing anything but, just resorting, to dropping her off somewhere. This was my best friend. We had already

been together for 10 years. I did finally find a place. We moved in a few

things after I realized she was not going to live alone. We spent a couple

of hours at the new place, when I heard this screaming coming from the

office area. The manager comes over and says she's calling the police.

It turns out, that Marzi, went over and said something to the lady. She

appeared to me, to be, a very unfriendly jackass that had little patience

and understanding of someone who needed help. The lady acted pretty

hateful, if you asked me.

   The police came, talked to Marzi and still did not help us admitt

her into a rehabilitation facility. The cop says to me that, at that point

in time, a person must prove that they are a homicidal or suicidal before

the police can be of assistance and / or arrest anyone. The only thing the cops helped us with that day was to insist that we move out right

then and there. This was my 3rd attempt to find Marz a place to live. She

was making it very difficult to get her into a new place. I had trouble

qualifying her to get a temporary dwelling. I didn't even have a steady job

at the time myself, so I wasn't in position to be excepted for an extended

stay either. The only thing we could get was a motel room.

The night, after they kicked Marz off the property, where I did

get the place there close to Bethany Home Rd, I drove us out to the Lake.

'Bartlett Lake', was, and still is the best resort area, with a marina.

If you don't have a boat and / or an Recreational Vehicle, ·there isn't very

many comfortable places to camp.

A few days before I finally did get us out of the Delgarosa apart-

ment, I got to the point where, I could not be, in the house at night. The

lights kept flickering, the volume of the TV was fluctuating, Marzi was going into the room, that I was trying to sleep in, and waking me up for

no practical reasons. The knot in my stomach was now making me feel

very ill. I finally got into the van, we had at the time, and decided to try

and sleep a few hours in another neighborhood. I got to sleep for once.

It seemed like minutes later that it was already morning, and a cop was

knocking on my window. I was parked on the side of some paranoid

whistle blower's house, that, had called the police. The officer turned out

to be a very nice and understanding guy, but he too basically said the

same thing. Marzi had to demonstrate a homicidal or suicidal character

before the law could intervene. That morning I realized I am going to

have to take charge and come up with a reasonable decision, that would

be a resolve, even if it meant just one day at a time.

When I returned to the house, a neighbor came out and said, that the police had come and hauled Marzi off to jail. I assumed, that, by me

not being there the cops finally saw that she needed help and would get

her into a rehabilitation facility. Marzi was suffering serious and

chronic depression which was probably responsible for her being so

affected by the entity. Something kept raining on our parade there in

that ridiculous apartment.

When I inquired about Marzi's status at the county, down town,

I found that she had spent the night with no blanket, no food, and the

staff didn't even make an effort to get her the meds that she was taking.

I drove down, waited on the steps outside the door, when they must have

released, 20 women. Marzi was so glad to see me that, the mean streak

she had been demonstrating, phased off at least 80%.

After being released from jail and being kicked off of two taxing properties, we finally did make it to the lake. It had been a dry year, and

the park service had the water table level down at least 25 feet. We drove

the van way down as close to the water as we could get, and found a

great place to build a fire and drink some beer. It was the first time I be-

came relaxed enough to eat, drink and be merry. That night, I fell asleep

and Marz claims she witnessed more than one bowl shaped flying objects

hovering over the lake, and, being chased by helicopters. It all sounded

like a hallucination to me, especially after the trauma we both had just

been through. When talking about it now, Marzi says, the memory of the

event is still clear as a bell. It's like Jackson Browne's songs: "You never

know what will be coming down, these days."

   After sleeping on the ground that night, I woke up with my mind

made up. I ended up getting another motel room that next afternoon. I got a break, but I was still in pretty bad shape. I took out some cash, rode

a bus to get our Ford Granada of which I had just painted. I also just had

the A/C compressor replaced. It was a great car. I had done extensive

work to the car over that past 3 years. There was a black woman that

was hanging around the dive motel, where Marz and I got the room. I

tried to get her to leave us alone. I didn't see her as a potential threat

or a problem. I installed a trailer hitch on the van. I found the title to the

car. I put $300 cash, the title and extra keys in the glove box. I gave Marzi

the keys to the Granada and I set off on foot. I caught a bus back to where

the van and the trailer was, and I split to Albuquerque.

    I had reached my breaking point. The decisions I made that day

were unsound. I was no longer capable of caring for someone who was

seriously affected by chemical imbalances. I was not able to make rational decisions. The forces of the evil that seemed to have been flagging and

succumbing us, was pulling me down like I was caught in a spiral funnel

of a sand dune. I had to use the only strength I had in reserve. The only

gas I had left in my tank was, borrowed, sheer determination.

Life throws a curve ball at us all once in awhile. Sometimes the

test can be impossible for some of us. I suppose I survived the blows

this time, only because I knew my limits, gauged by past experiences.

I finally composed myself when I reached the Elephant Butte

lake area, at Truth or Consequences. For the first time in two months,

I had some peace. I sat under the night sky and thanked my lucky stars

I was not swallowed up while living on a street called 'Delgarosa.'

14

THE REWARD

Wild horses dragged me away from Phoenix, it seemed. I was

so intent on sticking around. For years, I never had a reason to leave. I

kept getting on the wrong freeway. I think I felt like I didn't deserve to be

free of responsibility, because, in moment's exchange, I had a life again.

I stayed a couple of days at a big lake there in New Mexico. The

peace was overwhelming. When I hit Albuquerque that month, I did

find one of my old Los Luna buddies. After a couple of days with Berry,

I found a job, at an assembly line installation, at the west end of town.

The phone rang one day. When we answered the call, it dawned

on me,that, I had given out my friend's number to our best bud, Darla, in

Phoenix. We had known, Darla Swansen since 1997. She was home and

Marzi called us from there. I was surprisingly glad to hear her voice.

I knew she had become stabilized, and, that, she was her old self again.

I learned something about myself that day, and, more so, in the days that

followed. I learned just how much I had developed a need for a rock solid

home, and the stability of friends, that, really do care about me and, do,

value my presence. I ended up returning to Phoenix.

It really did take a large upheaval for me to truly appreciate, and

value, the bond I had with Marzi. The strength and the force of the entity

in that apartment on Delgarosa just about destroyed the best of us.

It completely manipulated Marzi's ability to stay in control.

The only advantage, I can think of, at that point before I left

Phoenix, during the days of our ordeal, was that, my headaches began to

get really serious. Lucky for me, I guess, the migraine headaches I began

to have at age 17, finally convinced me, that I was pouring fuel on the fire.

With a combination of the knot in my stomach, and getting sick from the

booze, I was really becoming a mess and, I had to *cut that juice*.

I mentioned, in earlier chapters, that, Olla had migraines. I think some-

times, when one inherits an ailment, it only gets worse with age. I haven't

said much about the migraine condition that has had a lot to do with my

lack of ambition. I do, want to add though, that, surely, I, would never

blame my headaches for any of my shortcomings, but, it is the one thing

that I have shared in common with Marzi. We both have cranial pain and

depression issues, and fortunately I've steered away from abusing alcohol.

Summer had already began the year I returned to Phoenix. It had only been 4 weeks. One of the first things that came through Marzi's lips

was, that, the Granada had been stolen. She let the black woman, at that

motel, that I mentioned before, use the car, who, whoops kept on goin'.

I was to learn very quickly, during the initial call, where. that left Marzi.

Three weeks had past since I left, & Marzi had literally been bare

foot, on the streets, that whole time. She lived with no money, transpor-

tation, nor shelter for almost 4 weeks. The cops had been monitoring

her, but, did not pick her up for lack of reason. There are hundreds of

homeless adults and adolescents everywhere in Phoenix now. 17 years

ago, it was just about as bad, per capita, in certain areas, here in the

southwest. She finally got the help she needed when she attempted to

get in to a building for shelter. The police did take her to a rehabilitation unit, thus being accessed for the mental illness she had been suffering,

and, the attack, at the Delgarosa apartment.

When I returned to Phoenix, and found Marzi, she explained that

she was stabilized in one treatment. For some reason, the system in 1999

was, just, not equipped and advanced enough to treat someone in an

emergency that was not really demonstrating homicidal or suicidal

tendencies. It had to be obvious that they were actually breaking in to

a facility, a house, or, appearing to be a threat to someone. She had been

treated and released in a couple of days. It was over night, from black,

to white. Marzi had already found herself, a month-to-month rental there

on Thomas Rd. I took the precious woman into my arms with a love so

deep and understanding. It amazed me that I left. Finding out what she

had endured, I must say, that, it was difficult to log it all, into a rational perspective. All I could do at that point, was to reassure Marzi

that she did not deserve, to go through all that. From there, the two of

us found jobs and a quiet place to live in just a few days.

We both bounced back, relatively quickly that summer, mostly

because, we were both still in our 40s. I thought I had seen it all, up 'til

then. The horror and the moral terror that some of us have to face can

surely test one's ability to access the strength that is within all of us. I

must say, that, this past episode was, some kind of challenge.

I want to emphasize the fact that, had I been in better financial

shape, I don't think,the run in, with the depression and the poltergeist,

would have overwhelmed us both, so strongly. Keep in mind that, if all

of us stopped moving around so much, due to family unrest and career

instability, most of us would not be moving into different apartments.

I am encouraging the young and old reading this book to take into account and value what your family has built up through the years.

Don't be so quick to leave it behind. Work things out, if you have dis-

agreements, try to love family members. Like Steven Seagal says in the

recent movie, 'End of a Gun': "The real treasures in life are about the

people that love you, and, are willing to take a bullet for you, while we

are fighting for common interests."

Reality is stranger than fiction. The events and the truth I en-

dured while at Durango, (my old wonderful high school), sent shock

waves through my spine the day Beth revealed that, Durango, is for

kids that have been in trouble with the law. It was in recent years that

she shared this news with me. Olla, never did say anything about that.

I was such an ignorant kid, suffering serious attention deficit problems,

that it's a wonder I even graduated. It never really aroused my curiosity when I was there, why, the kids were so mean. I had seen so much cruelty

all my elementary and early high school years that I figured the whole

time that, that it was nothing more than, but the norm. It wasn't like they

posted on the front gate, though, that, THIS IS A REFORM SCHOOL for

misfits. It's surprising, how the things that go on, the kids you hang with

and the choices you make in high school, have such a tremendous impact

on your entire life.

For years, I blamed my financial status to be the reason that I did

not attend my 25th year high school reunion. It has dawned on me, in re-

cent years, that the real problem was, pathetic. I had so many bullying,

and bad experiences, in two high schools, that, I just wanted to forget

about the whole mess, and never be reminded of those days again, which

now brings me to the next few lines I would like to share with you in this account of my, nutty family.

The truth about my father, Ansel, came as, some kind of shock.

It really surprised all of us. I took a job in Minnesota in 2011, and I got to

meet his sister and her son, Miles, for the first time in my life. He

cleared up all of the rumors, we had always heard, about our real dad and

his mysterious occupation. All Olla ever told us, was, that he traveled

from Minnesota to south Mexico, to preach the gospel. It turns out that,

what he was really doing, was driving down there, and bringing men

back across the border, for compensation. It never did make a lot of

sense to me, to believe, that someone would go to Mexico to sell God.

America has always been the best place, for that enterprise. Ansel, was

a good coyote. He got, while the was getting' good. He had purchased

a home in Los Angeles, to use, as a half way house, back in the day when human trafficking was basically excepted, as, not to be a big deal. He pro-

bably started that out to be an innocent gesture, managing to get the first

guy across, to go help build a church, or the like. He, no doubt, saw that

this could turn into a multilevel idea, and the sky became the limit. Just

take a look at today, what all that has become, be it good or bad.

In conclusion, you may recall my mentioning a few important

subjects in the introduction of this book. Yes, this has been a rocky and

confusing story along with, plenty of disgusting scenarios during the

forefront of my ridiculous life. I also mentioned that I believed that you

would benefit, if you do finish the book, and here's why...

When I ask, friends and coworkers, the question, "What is man's

most basic need?" This is a question that is a part of the 'Cigarest,'

quit smoking program I used in the 80s. It's a challenging question, and,

most come out, right away with, "the need for love-sex." Others try to think in practical terms, and say, something like, shelter, food & etc.

With most people, when they hear the word 'need' they think in terms

of money, for good reasons. Man's most basic need, is: 'THE NEED TO BE

COMFORTABLE.' For a large group of people the word money is the only

thing that would ever spell comfort, and that's OK too. I believe we all

know though, that, when you think about it, it takes quite a few subjects,

combined, to add up, to spell, the comfort zone.

If you yourself, indeed, did get bullied, or terrorized by a spouse,

then you know how difficult it is to feel comfortable. In my case, I was

abused by the bullies at school, bullies at the children's homes, and

ranches, then, by the parent. Sadly, the lack of money has very little to

to do with comfort when it comes down to who you are surrounded with.

I have seen families though, that have made good money, and because both parents topped off the cake with a whole lot of genuine love, un-

conditional, all family members usually did end up, under a very secure

financial blanket. These families simply collected all the ingredients of

the recipe. The same goes for the perfect formula to create a bully, or,

the child that gets bullied. It simply boils down to the power of *knowledge*

so... my question is this; are you waiting for the guy to come along

and share a big catch of fish with you, or, would you rather him teach you

his unique way, of how, he caught the fish?

You probably remember what I said, in chapter 2 about how im-

portant it is, to not criticize anyone, because in the end, the people that

learn to be happy and content, have utilized the knowledge. They were

not only influenced by a loving friend or family member. They were

shown the result and got to see, touch and experience it. How can you expect your child to want to plant, cultivate and nurture an idea when,

he or she, has never been given the chance to benefit from the hard

work? If, after being waylaid or stalled, and your child or your loved

one continues to be uninfluenced by his environment, they can easily go

off course again, and find it harder the second time to get back on track.

People can get criticized so harshly all because they usually end up

lacking drive and desire, early on. Thus, tremendous loss of productivity

each year is unmeasurable, all over the world. Imagine the resolve we

would see, if children were not so affected by, misunderstanding religion.

Kids can get the wrong message about other countries from parents,

peers, family, schools, evangelists and their military.

　The subject of people getting pushed around and bullied is a lot

more serious than a lot of us think, and want to believe. I will go as far, as to say, that kids that are influenced to blow up buildings, mutilation,

suicide and killing masses of victims, are rarely suffering a mental

illness. I think most can pass an IQ test, maybe even score high. The

truth is, the smarter they are, the more they would know that murder is

crazy, and, it surely ain't gonna give them, a better seat in the after life.

You may have read the book, or, saw the movie, 'Oh God.' I was

impressed with the author's idea when George Burns, (playing the role of

God), said, he did not perform miracles or magic. John Denver pleaded

and questioned, why doesn't God fix all these problems in the world...

George answered, reassuring him, that God has, from the beginning, been

generous with a wealth of endless supply of resources. He said also, that,

we need to stop criticizing and killing each other for personal gain, in the

name of segregation. This fixed mind set, gets started, when kids are growing up, pushing each other around and getting the wrong messages

from adults, adults that probably shouldn't of even had, and raised kids.

I would like to touch on a couple more ideas as I move toward the

closing of my endless dialog. I hope I haven't sounded like I have all the

answers. Everybody's got an opinion, and, the world is changing so fast,

that things get complicated.

As I have traveled to Ten-buck-Two and back several times, I have

seen one thing, for sure, that really does get you where it hurts. It's the

fact, that in most cases and situations which involve communication

where there is power, religion and philosophy, people continue to react

the same way every time. Like I have mentioned, more than once, officials

jump to the jungle-spring-into-action-mode, when it is no longer

necessary. What do you suppose is driving the dictator in North Korea to out do our military? There is more than one power, and, I encourage

you, to use your power, to be more of a benefit to the world. You can do it

if you visualize the end result. The phenomenal potential that lies within

people...There is an unbelievable amount of strength within you, that,

when unlocked and unleashed can heal more scars and hurt, than you

will ever know. The staggering importance of finding pleasure in your

work, is essential and more rewarding than you may imagine. You and I

are going to take advantage of the situation. BECAUSE, we were tortured,

and picked on to the point of nearing teenage suicide, we chose to sur-

vive and break through, taking advantage of the strength we developed

by hanging in there. Now, we can move forward and be productive, be-

cause we learned to understand the power of choice, and the power of

of the unconditional love and learning to love ourselves.

Time sure ain't waitin' around for anybody. Sometimes we only

get one chance. I sure do try to get it right the first time these days.

It's becoming a very challenging world. We gotta be ready and, best

equipped, with enough, and, the right kind of ammunition.

Marzi and I, have continued living in Arizona ever since I re-

turned in 1999. That last episode of madness, at Delgarosa, took such a

toll on the both of us, that, since then we haven't had the energy, rhyme

or reason to up-root. Everything I have learned in my life, spells the fact

that, there never was a greener pasture.

I am going to exit this final chapter with the most important

reason I decided to share my story and experiences. The magic and the

miracles that I have seen in my travels, is when, someone discovers how

to appreciate the beauty of being alive without pain. If you have a shelter

from the storm and food in your house with an income, these are the magical ingredients for a life with a promise. The biggest mistake that

warriors like us could ever make, is to believe someone, that tells you

that, you are powerless over addiction. You can make adjustments in your

life to overcome depression after being bullied. That's not to say that

you should not reach out for help. I just want to make sure that you un-

derstand the magic in the power of *choice*. When you are sure about

what you need to do, or change, it is entirely up to you. There is plenty of

programs and professionals that can aide you, in your decision.

I haven'tt said a whole lot, nor have I attempted to advise on the

bully subject. I will say, that, it is one thing to be bullied when kids have

good parents around, in a functional home. It is quite another, when,

children are alone to figure out how to handle the affair without help.

This is when it gets dangerous. I suppose you could say I was influenced, to turn the other cheek, in spite of the burning, bottled up anger I had to

control. I learned to keep in mind that my health was very important, and

I had hope, if, and when I was healthy. He who has hope, has more than

most of us realize. Hope is a weapon for me, and my primary ammunition

involved learning to love myself enough to begin to love others. So fight-

ing back now with, real love, has become my grandest weapon when deal-

ing with opposition. Love can be a very powerful tool. Men have been

going to war in search of something for a long time. If anybody ever

found it, we would all be at home to stay, by now.

I can't emphasize enough how important it is for children, now

days, to pay special attention to the message learned in the Martial Arts.

Whether, or not, kids take classes in the arts, a good trainer will be very

clear about the idea that when we hate, fear is a large factor. People hate because they don't understand what they don't know. The more you

know about the importance of allowing love to be the ignition in the

style of confrontation, you put out the fire of hate, before it gets started.

There is a lot at stake here for, you and me both. Our success depends a

lot on the manner of how we hang in there to fight these battles regard-

less of age or gender. We need allies, not more enemies. What we accom-

plish these days, is depending more and more, on how we spend our

precious time that is ticking away. It seems to gain speed as we age.

I wrote this book, mainly to get couple of things across to young

kids, having the many growing pains we all have. I can't say it enough.

Please, don't do what I did. Sure, I got pushed around and was made to

feel inferior and worthless, but life goes on. Think about what is really important. Don't allow people to continue to intimidate you. Arm your-

self with being crystal clear about what you want. If you are still in high

school, communicate your fears. Just do what you need to do, to hang on,

to your dreams when kids try to divert your attention. To some degree,

your high school years can be the most important and precious spaces of

time. Your reactions, to confrontations, with, not so friendly people, can

can surely count for how effective you are going be in the career and/or

the life style you choose. This is when we begin to develop values, and

ideas. If you are still living with your parents, and, you may not be getting

along so well, try to remember, people are not born knowing how to

raise children. You may be stuck with a single parent who is really strug-

gling to survive. Regardless of how many parents, brothers and sisters or friends you have, remember, to value them. Go home and give them

all and big hug, and, tell them that you sincerely love them. Family can be

one of your greatest assets, now and in the future. They can help you

with your struggle to find out where you fit, and, what you decide to do.

Again, above all else, don't do like me. The adults I grew up with just

did not know, how to handle, a bad day. We, as you well know, as human

beings, are going to have challenging days. Adults in my past had the

tendency to say, they were depressed on a bad day. They believed it was

more than just an uninspired, normal, human behavioral pattern that

gets the best of us from time to time. You, are going to be influenced by

this behavior because we all need to vent our feelings. I can't tell you how

important it is to understand the need for the night, so, you can recognize day. If there was no evil, we would not know how to identify good. If we

never got bullied by all of these jackass jerks, we would never have

learned to appreciate and identify the wonderful, creative, open minded,

selfless, dynamic and loving people out here. These are the kind of

strangers that helped to save my sorry ass. Did I learn the formula to the

global configuration? Probably not. I just found the things that compute.

The question I have for you now is, what did you hope to get out of this

book? Did you have expectations that you feel were not necessarily

touched on, nor addressed? If you are still not feeling like your problem

is continuing to be unique to you, join the club. You have friends on this

block. The trick, is to stay off the cell block.

The one thing that I, as an individual, have managed to pull off

is; I never have got arrested. I have not spent a single night locked up

for drug charges, nor for losing my cool. In a way that makes me a good candidate for writing this book, but, on the other hand some of you might

be thinking, that, I just don't know what it's like. To be brought up amidst

such crime infested cities, that, seem to be impossible to function, it can

be so hard, but, it depends on the how you perceive the present situation.

Do you wanna engage in methods to make it worse, or, do you see how

you could benefit to help to fix it? You have continued to read this book

because you were bullied and pushed to your limit. I am asking you now,

to make a choice. Are you going to go to church, drum a magician or pay a

fortune teller? Will you look for a kind of transcending invisible life

changing external force to magically solve all the violent an selfish pro-

blems that surround you? Again, you may be saying, "I don't need

another lecture," and I don't blame you. We are all sick to death of the results that arise due to being made to feel like we don't deserve to be

included in the clan. The answers to this dilemma don't come easy.

Let's face it, people who are tormented and pushed around for

years, are without a doubt going to be harder to get along with. They may

have a bad temper, and, can have trouble making a living. Because, we did

get a raw deal though, we learned to make our own luck, and did not

expect, nor, rely on hand outs from friends or family.

As you join the ranks of the warriors that survived the years of

peers, and so called friends, that needed to put you down so they would

look good, please remember one thing. From here on out, no matter what

road you get on, where you want to go, or, what you want to be, the

answer is simple. You just have to choose to be the kind of person that

makes things happen.

Since I arrived at the point in my life when drugs and alcohol no longer did the trick like they used to, I've done a flip. Now days, I have

become addicted to concrete accomplishments. In other words, I simply

have to be engaged in a project, and, stick with it to the bitter end, finish

it, or, die trying. I can't say enough, about, how satisfying it can be.

The endless reward in, *finding pleasure in your toil*. Hang on to

to those words. To love your work, to take pride in holding on to your

dignity, just may only include, maintaining your status by keeping your

job. This can be a lot more than others have. When you do learn to take

into account how precious your body/mind really is, you will surely

find an endless, magnificent compensation, and countless resources. The

degree of reward that a person feels, arriving at these levels of compre-

hension, can keep us all excited. I'm probably about to make you sick

by now, though, with all of this glorified rhetoric. I just simply, can not, emphasize enough, how important, it really is, to refuse, to let your un-

fortunate past, sabotage your connection with people. Friends, family

and business associates are essential. It is extremely important that you

understand that you have developed issues, with your ability, to be a

leader and / or a follower. You have been rejected and criticized in such

a manner, that, you are uncomfortable, with making commitments. This

is one of our largest stumbling blocks. This is why I have **struck out** so

severely at the greatest opportunities. They will work only, if you handle

yourself, in a way that you can be *receptive*, to these chances of lifetime.

Believe me, it takes, without a doubt, an unconditional joint effort.

This IS the future. We are living in a very simple world, but,

man has complicated things. Things have changed so rapidly that it

really does require a lot of meditative thought these days. Keep in mind, though, that the ingredients are all out there. If you can love yourself

enough to continue to love others, people will be attracted to your ideals.

Remember too, that some people are simply born to lose. Others have to

work at it... We either make a hell of trying to get to heaven, or, we make

a heaven of the hell we live in.

If you will set your luggage down for a minute and try to forget.

Let's set aside the nagging and damaging memories and trust nature to

divulge some, easier to swallow information. It is possible to find, all the

ingredients, that ad up, to cook the whole tamale.

The earth, does share many ways to, not only cope, but, to

break through to the power, the power to find a sense of direction. You

can fit in, and, yes, you can feel special without counting on magic

tricks. It is doable to like yourself and live in harmony.

Remember that, the quality of your life, depends, on the quality of your decisions. So let's make the right choices.

For such a challenging environment, in the end, I believe we

would all surely agree, that this is a wonderful planet, and it is ten times

better than living on Mars*

BULLY WITH A GUN

Words & Music By:
Lou Enzo Mayson

Everybody's on the run
looking for a warm place in the sun
But, when I find My chosen one
Am I gonna need to carry a Gun?

Yeah, when my song is finally sung
I want to be singing like I won
But, when the day is surely done
Am I gonna need to carry a Gun?

I just want to have some fun
I just want to see the sun
But, I don't want to have to be the one
To pick out people with a gun...

There's a Bully with a gun!
And he surely ain't the only one
What's he gonna teach his son?
There's a Bully with a Gun

Printed in the United States
By Bookmasters